Hugo Wolf
and the Wagnerian Inheritance

In spite of growing interest in the songs of Hugo Wolf, there is still a lack of serious critical discussion of the nature of his achievements, in particular his relationship to Richard Wagner. Wolf has been regarded as a composer who followed the style and aesthetics of Wagnerian music drama without question, while writing in a genre often seen as less challenging than the symphony or opera. This book re-examines the evidence concerning Wolf's responses to Wagner and Wagnerism, and suggests ways in which he voiced his criticism through song and through his one completed opera, *Der Corregidor*. This opens up new insights into the kind of impact Wagner had on those following in his wake, and into the complexity and subtlety of the late nineteenth-century Lied. From this perspective, Wolf emerges as a persuasive and articulate figure, of wider musical and artistic significance than has yet been recognised.

AMANDA GLAUERT is a senior lecturer at the Royal Academy of Music, and has contributed articles to the *New Grove Dictionary of Opera, Wagner in Performance* (Yale University Press) and *The Cambridge Companion to Beethoven* (Cambridge University Press, forthcoming).

Hugo Wolf
and the Wagnerian Inheritance

AMANDA GLAUERT

PUBLISHED BY THE PRESS SYNDICATE OF THE UNIVERSITY OF CAMBRIDGE
The Pitt Building, Trumpington Street, Cambridge CB2 1RP, United Kingdom

CAMBRIDGE UNIVERSITY PRESS
The Edinburgh Building, Cambridge CB2 2RU, United Kingdom
40 West 20th Street, New York, NY 10011-4211, USA
10 Stamford Road, Oakleigh, Melbourne 3166, Australia

First published 1999

Printed in the United Kingdom at the University Press, Cambridge

Typeset in Photina 10/13½ [SE]

A catalogue record for this book is available from the British Library

Library of Congress cataloguing in publication data

Glauert, Amanda.
    Hugo Wolf and the Wagnerian inheritance / Amanda Glauert.
        p.   cm.
    Includes bibliographical references and index.
    ISBN 0 521 49637 3 (hardback)
    1. Wolf, Hugo, 1860–1903 – Criticism and interpretation.
    2. Wagner, Richard, 1813–1883 – Influence.   I. Title.
    ML410.W8G53   1998
    782.42168′092 – dc21   98-21453 CIP

ISBN 0 521 49637 3 hardback

Contents

❖

Contents

Acknowledgements

Many people have helped in the long germination of this project – from the challenging work I undertook with Robin Holloway in the late 1970s, to the thesis I completed at London University, to the present book. I am very grateful to those who encouraged me at various stages, including my doctoral supervisor Paul Banks, Peter Franklin, Julian Rushton, William Kinderman and Barry Millington. The present book has benefited greatly from the stimulating criticism of Laurence Dreyfus, as well as from the responses of my colleagues at the Royal Academy of Music – particularly Sarah Callis. Susan Youens has been an enthusiastic and inspiring ally in the cause of Wolf research, and I also would like to thank the Wolf and Mahler enthusiasts I have uncovered among students at the Academy, and at Colchester Institute where previously I lectured for many years. Penny Souster has been most patient and encouraging as an editor – qualities for which I also have to thank my husband, Simon Thompson.

Acknowledgements

Introduction

❧

If we were seeking a context to help in understanding the music of Hugo Wolf, then one might wish for a less problematic one than his relationship to Wagner and the Wagnerian inheritance. As critics, we usually seek to go beyond composers' efforts at self-validation, however eloquent and moving they may be; one might say it is a sign of our serious regard that we do not simply accept their acknowledged and immediate stories of influence and intention, but look also for the unspoken aspects which reveal the human engagement behind their work. Yet it was precisely such critical activity that Wagner sought to bypass, offering his own view of music history that extended beyond personal actions; he purported to account for much of the broader working of culture and bring this also within a single fixed perspective. More striking still, Wagner made a conscious exhibition of his struggles for artistic coherence and identity both in his writings and in the music dramas themselves, offering himself as his own critic – an artist of complete awareness and control.

Wagner's claims, as the philosopher Friedrich Nietzsche recognised, helped provoke a crisis in criticism that we are still addressing today, a crisis that gives urgency to the uncovering of multiple layers in the interpretation of Wagner's work and in the pursuit of musical meaning in general. However, we have still tended to underestimate the impact of Wagner in forming our view of those composers who followed in his wake. There were obvious temptations for post-Wagnerian composers to grab prestige for themselves, by claiming an association with Wagner's cultural aims and with his stylistic solutions. It was tempting for them also to seek immunity from criticism, particularly when they were struggling to assimilate the musical and aesthetic innovations of works such as Wagner's *Tristan und Isolde* and were in danger of losing their artistic balance. Certain contemporary commentators connived in promoting such composers as the 'Wagner of the Lied' or 'Wagner of the Symphony', partly out of concern for their vulnerability. Wolf and Bruckner, for example, were seen as dangerously separated from the public, pushing the Lied and symphony in new directions that sometimes seemed to make little sense to the uninitiated. They were also seen as naive and powerless in social and even artistic terms, incapable of articulating an entirely coherent and independent response to the complexities of the time. Critics believed that their music needed to be seen against the external aesthetic frame of Wagner himself, as though he were the final magnetic point for all their artistic endeavour.[1] What Wolf and Bruckner distinctively offered, in the eyes of their supporters, was the simplicity of genius, the ability to gloss over the contradictions of transferring the habits of music drama to symphony or song through their 'inspiration'. The much-told stories of Bruckner's religious devotion, composing to the glory of God, were matched by those of Wolf's single-minded zeal for poetry. The poet and playwright Hermann Bahr's descriptions of Wolf's trance-like reading of his favourite poets became adopted as a literal picture of the compositional processes of his songs. As Bahr wrote in 1898, in the preface to the Hugo Wolf-Verein's volume of critical essays on the composer, from out of his rapt state Wolf was able to create 'the verse's own music, the music that lives in them, that must always have been there, and that he just allows to sound forth'.[2] One is reminded of the famous image of Bruckner listening to *Tristan und Isolde* with his eyes closed, taking in nothing of the story of the poetic drama, as though this might allow him to absorb Wagner's music drama and transform it directly into symphony.

One knows, however, that Bruckner's symphonies actually underwent complex processes of revision, as the composer struggled to assert himself against the more conventional Wagnerian instincts of his friends and advisers the Schalk brothers.[3] And any serious consideration of Wolf's work soon reveals that his songs never conformed straightforwardly to the expectations set by a poem's content or structure. His poetic interpretations bear the signs of processes of negotiation and reflection that allow little to be taken for granted, least of all Wagner's assertion that 'poetry is the man, music the woman'. Wagner claimed that his music dramas had absorbed the nature of symphony and song, and that his aesthetic formula for the relationships between music and poetry could transcend the boundaries of genre. However, in his own artistic creations Wolf sought to reawaken listeners to the distinctiveness of song, and to the greater variety and subtlety possible within its more detailed aesthetic relationships, if only his listeners were prepared to appreciate them. On the evidence of the songs' reception, it seems critics have been surprisingly reluctant to give up their fictions of Wolf as a single-minded fanatic,[4] continuing to see him as following the authority of Wagner and 'the poet' without question. The views of Josef Schalk, and other Wolfian critics connected to the Viennese Wagner Society, were inevitably affected by their concerns for Wagner himself; to them Wolf was one of the most significant links in the spreading of Wagner's influence, precisely because of the possibility of tracing a spiritual affinity to Wagner through poetry. Any notion that Wolf might question the nature of that link would have been deeply disturbing to them. For it would have undermined important aspects of Wagner's claims to have diagnosed the present 'needs' of music – the need for all music to be led by an inseparable 'love-bond' with a poet. Without the corroboration of other composers' experiences, such claims would begin to seem like Wagner's purely personal perceptions, no more valid than anyone else's.

In the late nineteenth century not many Wolfian critics were ready to accept such a collapse of cultural certainties. But nowadays the unravelling of Wagner's claims has begun to reveal the 'many Wagners', the shifting aesthetic viewpoints, in his work; so much so that his role as a founder of modernism can jostle with perceptions of him as a conservative or post-modernist with surprising ease.[5] And yet there is still a reluctance to prise Wolf free of past cultural labels or to delve too closely into the nature of his Wagnerian discipleship. It is as though we fear that, unlike Wagner's, his music might not survive the collapse of a monolithic view of history or of a certain aesthetic vision. In particular, we underestimate the potential of the Lied as a vehicle for aesthetic complexity, thinking that the genre must remain one-dimensional as an intimate and lyrical reflection of composers themselves and their immediate expressive intentions.

Yet the more we know of Wolf, of his life and aspirations, the more difficult it becomes to align him in any way with the simple labels that have been applied to him. He clearly knew that it was a dubious honour to be dubbed a successor to Wagner, and that any such position brought him conflict as much as glory. He was both drawn to Wagner and repelled by him; his feelings and intentions were often changing, as one can indeed see reflected on the surface of his work, in his obvious shifting of style and approach from song to song. As one delves more deeply into Wolf's detailed responses to the Lied's disciplines of form and content, questions about his relationship to Wagner and the expectations of his time emerge almost of their own accord. One also begins to appreciate just how much his artistic solutions defy easy labels. Far from needing to protect Wolf from the many changes in our view of Wagner, we should be trying to catch up with the complexity of view his songs offer. They undoubtedly confirm our modern suspicions that the Wagnerian inheritance was the most challenging and problematic of burdens, and yet they also snatch an integrity and clarity from the midst of conflict which remain the more precious for the difficult context in which they were achieved.

Chapter one

'Music of the future'? The nature of the Wagnerian inheritance

❧

When in 1900 the famous Viennese critic Eduard Hanslick labelled Mahler, Strauss and Wolf together as the 'Musical Secession',[1] he could hardly have found a less congenial group of bedfellows. Wolf thought Strauss's music affected madness,[2] Mahler hated Wolf's songs for their emphasis on 'de-cla-ma-tion',[3] while Strauss and Mahler respected each other across a gulf of mutual incomprehension.[4] One might say that Hanslick was revealing his ignorance of the complexity of post-Wagnerian movements and relying on the simplest of cultural distinctions. For it is true that Mahler, Strauss and Wolf can be quickly identified as those who believed in the artist as revolutionary hero – as against artists who placed emphasis on respect for the past. If Hanslick still defined artistic 'secession' in 1900 as leaving behind any commonly agreed criteria of beauty, demanding the freedom to establish one's own standards of truth and value, then all three would be 'secessionists' without question. But then so would be almost every other well-known Austro-German composer of the late nineteenth century, except perhaps for the notable case of Brahms. Brahms's music certainly continued to focus on the power of Classical forms and technique; but as Schoenberg pointed out in his essay 'Brahms the Progressive' this direct continuity with the past was a complex and individual achievement. In Austria or Germany in the late nineteenth century any norms of musical expectation were more easily filtered through Wagner than Brahms, but with confusing consequences, for Wagner's example tended to set all notions of tradition, belonging and secession on their heads.

One of Wagner's greatest acts of public daring was to question the coherence of Beethoven's late works *and* offer himself as their 'redeemer'. With this he dramatically reversed the usual notions of dependence within a tradition, of authority flowing from a master to his disciple. For Wagner suggested that Beethoven's works relied on him for their artistic validation, rather than the other way around. He proposed that Beethoven's symphonies could only be fully understood through his recreating their conception in his music dramas; he offered his own works as

Beethoven's 'deeds of music' made visible.[5] Wagner said Beethoven was moving towards a recognition of his symphonic music's insufficiency when he added a text to the Ninth Symphony. But the older composer was only imperfectly aware of his artistic needs and intentions; Wagner must speak for him in order to bring out their true tendency. Once he had thus secured Beethoven's artistic integrity, as he put it, Wagner claimed his rights as Beethoven's heir and his own place within tradition.

Such a 'tradition' was now transparently presented as an artistic fiction of the composer himself, conceived in a Promethean spirit of self-reliance. Many of Wagner's music dramas depict this same idea of a 'hero' seeking out his own history and realising it against all the odds; it is acted out in the relationships between Walther and Hans Sachs, of Siegfried, Siegmund and Wotan, and of Parsifal, Amfortas and Titurel. In *Die Meistersinger*, *Parsifal* and *Der Ring* Wagner confirmed that the 'hero' also needed the affirmation of a wider community to recognise his claims to be the heir of a spiritual heritage. Even Siegfried needed to have his role and lineage laid out before gods and men by Brünnhilde at the end of *Götterdämmerung*. Wagner thus revealed his awareness of what a living tradition should be, a drawing together of public and individual perspectives. But having shown this awareness, the composer seemed to consider himself free from all further cultural validation. Once established in his self-sufficient and timeless representations of the processes of tradition, Wagner seemed to feel he might describe his dramas as 'Music of the Future' without fear of ironic reprisal from his detractors. Advocates of Wagner's work soon understood that the slogan was essentially a relative term, referring to the cultural ideal presented in the music dramas themselves, rather than to the uncertain matter of how musical tastes might change after Wagner. Hostile critics enjoyed pointing out how Wagner's work did not produce successful followers in the usual sense, but only weak imitations with little artistic strength of their own. However, this too reinforced the particular nature of Wagner's cultural diagnosis. For the composer believed that significant artistic creations could only arise from acts of daring similar to his own appropriation and completion of Beethoven. He warned his followers not to copy only the external patterns of his music dramas, but to address a similarly pressing artistic 'need'.[6] Yet he was clearly confident that nobody would dare to find his own work incomplete or need to propose a further future for his music dramas.

Indeed in case his links to Beethoven might make the line of artistic 'tradition' seem too short-term, raising expectations of another artistic conqueror on the immediate horizon, Wagner encouraged writers in the journal *Bayreuther Blätter* to take to the 'high ground' and trace his heritage back to Luther and Dürer.[7] It was partly in response to such calls that Nietzsche identified Wagner's music dramas with the recovery of Greek classical tragedy in his *The Birth of Tragedy from the Spirit of Music* of 1872. In his essay 'Richard Wagner in Bayreuth' of 1876, Nietzsche described how Wagner asked him to:

help me . . . discover that culture whose existence my music, as the rediscovered language of true feeling, prophesies; reflect that the soul of music now wants to create for
itself a body, that it seeks its path through all of you to visibility in movement, deed,
structure and morality![8]

Note that there was no suggestion here that the 'soul of music' might need further
nurturing or kindling, but only that what had been completed in the music dramas,
on behalf of all music, might be recognised in other spheres. Nietzsche's vision of a
living culture which he unfolded in his essay 'On the Uses and Disadvantages of
History for Life' of 1874 could indeed be taken as a tribute to Wagner. For he suggested there that a 'strong' artist must

be able to assimilate and appropriate the things of the past . . . That which such a nature
cannot subdue it knows how to forget; it no longer exists, the horizon is rounded and
closed, and there is nothing left to suggest that there are people, passions, teachings,
goals lying beyond it. And this is a universal law: a living thing can be healthy, strong and
fruitful only when bounded by a horizon; if it is incapable of drawing a horizon around
itself, and at the same time too self-centred to enclose its own view within that of
another, it will pine away slowly or hasten to its timely end.[9]

The kind of balance which Nietzsche outlined – between artistic self-determination
and self-forgetfulness, timeless isolation and wider cultural awareness – might have
encouraged Wagner in believing he could encapsulate a living culture in his music
dramas. Like Nietzsche, he professed a dislike of 'monumentality' in art, condemning
the fixedness which results from a fear of history and the desire to prevent change. He
once wrote to Liszt 'Children! create something *new*! something *new*! and again something *new*!'[10] – words which later became the slogan of the Wagnerians in the
Viennese Wagner Society and were used to justify their support of Bruckner and
Wolf.[11] To the Viennese Wagnerians, these composers were 'true fruit from the
Master's stem',[12] confirming in their eyes how Wagner's creative influence would
continue to spread. However, the quasi-religious terminology employed here, remi-
niscent of Jesus's references to himself as the vine and his disciples as the branches in
chapter 15 of John's gospel, points up an extreme aspect in the view of tradition associated with Wagner. For he claimed like Christ to have done everything necessary for
'salvation'; and others came also to believe that a living culture was ensured, provided the music dramas themselves, and they alone, remained the focus of attention.
Even Wagner's command to composers to 'create something *new*!' might be taken to
reflect primarily upon his own claims to creativity, as though he were echoing God's
words in Revelation – 'Behold, I make all things new.'

Nietzsche once remarked that Wagner cared little about how musicians under his
influence actually composed:

[I]t is plain that Wagner is not very much concerned whether composers from now on
compose in a Wagnerian manner or whether they compose at all; indeed, he does what
he can to destroy the unfortunate current belief that a school of composers must now

necessarily attach itself to him. Insofar as he exercises a direct influence on present-day musicians he tries to instruct them in the art of grand execution.[13]

Throughout his later life Wagner was obsessed with the need to found a singing school, to establish 'a *stylistic tradition* by means of which his work could live on unalloyed from one age to the next'.[14] Cosima remained true to Wagner's wishes, a singing institute being finally opened in 1892. Yet the Bayreuth circle admitted that Wagner would need to become identified with composers as well as performers if his influence was to continue to grow.[15] One critic close to the circle, Arthur Seidl, decided that composers after Wagner could only be interpreted as a 'school' in a special sense. In his pamphlet 'Hat Richard Wagner eine Schule hinterlassen?' (Has Richard Wagner Left a School behind Him?) of 1892, Seidl likened post-Wagnerian composers to the tail left behind by a comet, with no power or will of its own, reflecting the comet's glory but creating nothing of itself. Any innovation they might seem to offer was still an essentially passive reflection of the comet's light and strength.[16] On the other hand this conferred a certain spiritual prestige upon composers. Provided they held enough of a stylistic bond with Wagner Seidl welcomed them into the ranks of the 'modern', for he judged them then to be an indivisible part of Wagner's expanding world-view. He looked for the immediate echoes of Wagner's work in others, without making subtle distinctions over the aesthetic use composers might make of them. For instance he decided that Bruckner could not be included in a Wagnerian school because of his symphonies' lack of definite poetic content,[17] even though Josef Schalk argued in the *Bayreuther Blätter* that Bruckner's exalting of the purely musical was close to Goethe's search for the 'eternal feminine', the spiritual realm which Wagner believed united his text and music in *Tristan und Isolde*.[18] Likewise, Seidl included Hugo Wolf in his Wagnerian list in 1892, but crossed him out in 1900 as a 'Rückblick' – a look backwards – saying there were now too many Schubertian features in his songs.[19]

Seidl was often criticised for his superficiality and for judging from externals only, as for example by the Wagnerian aesthetician Friedrich von Hausegger.[20] But in fact his judgements came from a deep-seated and, in some ways, penetrating view of the all-embracing tendency of Wagner's art. Hans von Wolzogen, the editor of the *Bayreuther Blätter*, expressed his heartfelt gratitude on the publication of 'Hat Richard Wagner eine Schule hinterlassen?' for receiving an answer to what 'following Wagner' without 'eclipsing Wagner' might mean. According to Wolzogen, Seidl confirmed that the Wagnerians of the Bayreuth circle were 'on the right path and can do no better than to continue to walk and work together, always on the same path'.[21] Wolzogen's notion of 'a right path' chimes in with the language of modernism. But, in fact, Wolzogen had an avowedly reactionary tendency and was far more blatant than Seidl in conceiving the path to the future as circular, designed to lead steadily back round the circumference of Wagner's music dramas themselves. One can see the editor's conservative effect upon the *Bayreuther Blätter* from 1892 onwards as the 'safer' figures of Siegfried Wagner, Engelbert Humperdinck and Martin Plüddemann, those who had an obvious and immediate connection with Wagner, begin to dominate the journal's review pages, at the expense of more adventurous composers such as Hugo Wolf.

One might wonder what had happened to Wagner's aspirations for cultural domination, once the discussion over the future seemed in danger of becoming restricted to questions of how one might transfer aspects of Wagner's techniques directly to fairy-tale opera or the ballad. The Wagnerians who wrote in the pages of *Bayreuther Blätter* seemed to have opted for smaller fields to conquer, advising would-be followers to keep away from the grandeur of music drama itself and try smaller *Gesamtkunstwerke*, such as the Lied or ballad.[22] The attempts to imitate Wagner too directly had led to many artistic disasters though, as already discussed, these would not in themselves have affected Wagner's credibility if certain doubts about the claims he had made had not begun to arise from among his own supporters. For Nietzsche's famous 'betrayal' of Wagner, as the Bayreuth circle termed it, began to have far-reaching consequences for the reception of Wagner's music even among Wagnerians. Nietzsche first voiced doubts over whether Wagner could truly be called a 'strong' man of history after 1874, when he witnessed the collapse of Wagner's Bayreuth plans.[23] But the 'rounded horizon' of Wagner's *Gesamtkunstwerk* began to seem even more like an illusion to Nietzsche after he had actually experienced the first Bayreuth festival in 1876. He recognised the composer's will to conquer his audience: his music was indeed 'terrifyingly distinct, just as if it were trying to make itself heard by deaf people'. But to Nietzsche the heightened gestures of the *Ring* revealed a 'volubility with nothing to say'.[24]

Thus Nietzsche was not only distressed that Wagner had sought to realise their cultural ideals through a vulgar concert-going institution; he also came to believe that the composer had always been acting a part and had never been able to share those ideals in the first place.[25] One remnant of the grand vision survived, for Nietzsche still claimed that Wagner was truly reflecting the currents of his time, even if the message that he saw coming out of Bayreuth had to be taken as the opposite of the one Wagner proclaimed. According to Nietzsche, 'We are witnessing the death agony of the *last great art*: Bayreuth has convinced me of this.'[26] The figure of 'Wagner the magician', setting out to trick his audiences with hollow images of power, could only be 'redeemed' by holding up the figure of 'Wagner the naive' – the one who had been able to reveal the general cultural weakness by blindly following through his own instincts.[27]

The Viennese critic Max Graf took up these contradictory pictures of Wagner in his book *Wagner-Probleme* of 1900. He suggested that as Nietzsche's critique took effect, Wagnerians had to relinquish their images of 'the mighty German singer . . . the master of a strong and glorious art' and begin to see him as the singer of many sorrows, mourning his inner weakness.[28] For to Graf, Wagner's art was 'a scattering of powers towards the limits of experience and then a yearning for their reunification'. He could not be compared to Goethe or Beethoven, who created from a strong centre, producing roots, stem and crown from the same source.[29] Post-Wagnerians must turn away from Wagner to find their own strength as artists:

> With deep emotion and awe, we, the avant-garde of a new generation, turned away from Wagner's picture and after moments of fear and trembling stepped out together and with heads held high towards our own world, our own sun.[30]

The triumphalism of these final words contrasts somewhat strangely with the accompanying suggestions of emotional disturbance. Graf saw Nietzsche as the leader of this new avant-garde; he believed the philosopher had conquered Wagner and taken his place as the true heir to Beethoven and Goethe.[31] But Graf also recognised that Nietzsche had not left Bayreuth with 'the calm step of a conqueror, but delirious, orgiastic, drunk from the fight – it was his last'.[32]

Both Graf and Nietzsche wished to make positive suggestions of ways forward for the post-Wagnerian generation, while also seeming aware that they were in danger of pointing them into a cultural vacuum. Graf directed his readers back to Beethoven's 'Ode to Joy' and a belief in the 'beauty of life',[33] as though one might return to a pre-Wagner innocence and retrace the steps of a healthy cultural tradition. But it is hard to imagine how any composer could openly bid for such a spiritual heritage and yet avoid Wagner's deception of hiding personal aspirations behind claims to represent a wider tradition. Brahms certainly succeeded in avoiding any deceptive claims, keeping rigorously to practical questions of technique and form. But then neither Graf nor Nietzsche was content with what they saw as his limited cultural perspective. Graf called Brahms an 'artistic recluse', morosely watching and standing aside from the 'struggling developments of the new spirit'.[34] Strauss and Mahler fitted more easily into Graf's hope for a renewed revolution. The critic commented optimistically on Mahler's performances of Beethoven's Ninth Symphony, saying they opened a new world of feeling, beyond the one already opened by Wagner's performances.[35] And in his composing, as seen in the Second Symphony, Graf said Mahler knew how to approach the symphonic form with level-headedness, even while giving it a new spiritual clothing.[36]

Such appreciation and understanding seldom came Mahler's way, particularly so early in his career; critics usually balked at the uncomfortable jostling of public and personal associations in his symphonies. Yet such juxtapositions could be seen positively within Graf's world-view; they prevented any sign of the composer imitating Wagner's pretensions and trying to swallow the Classical heritage entirely into his own artistic makeup. Instead, Mahler clearly encouraged his listeners to reflect upon the possibilities of continuity with tradition, deliberately interrupting their expectations of Beethovenian formal development with irrational contrasts which were never entirely smoothed away. The seemingly endless waiting upon symphonic closure in the last movement of the Second Symphony remains as potent an impression in the listener's mind as the final chorus with its self-consciously Beethovenian message of resolution. While each impression reinforces the effect of the other and belongs, as Mahler would put it, within the same 'symphonic world', the two impressions of the finale do not entirely add up. The 'world' of the symphony is represented as being beyond the artist's immediate formal control, in a way that reflects ironically upon Wagner's formulation of enclosed and self-fulfilling 'worlds' in his music dramas. Without overt stylistic or spiritual reference to Wagner, Mahler succeeded in disclosing the problems surrounding his music dramas' claim upon the future. Indeed Adorno believed that Mahler created his music entirely out of an awareness of cultural collapse, building a language out of fragments and echoes of the past.[37]

From such a perspective, Hanslick's label of 'secessionist' sits quite ironically upon Mahler, since his symphonies suggest that the separation of the artist from tradition, even from all ideas of tradition, is an inescapable part of the post-Wagnerian consciousness. Such a distance was given, rather than being chosen or created by the heroic will of the composer himself. Echoes of the artist as 'hero' occur quite often in Mahler's symphonies, but they are treated to different kinds of radical denial. In the Sixth Symphony Mahler paints a picture of the 'artist-hero' wishing to impose a will and direction upon his work, but this is shown to lead to the collapse of almost all symphonic utterance. In the Ninth Symphony's first movement the musical continuity is provocatively pieced together from the returns to the opening fragments, rather than from the heroically assertive contrasting sections which overtly strive for a long-term musical goal.

Apart from his offering an ironic reflection upon Wagner, one might also detect in Mahler's works a dig at the sometimes hyperbolic musical language of Strauss, his supposed 'comrade-in-arms'.[38] However, Strauss was not above creating his own ironic reflections of the hero-worship bestowed on him by the public. In 1892 Arthur Seidl already recognised Strauss's symphonic poem *Tod und Verklärung* as a supremely successful example of the work of the post-Wagnerian 'school'.[39] The matching of stylistic innovation with a clearly appropriate poetic programme allowed Strauss to emulate the completeness of the *Gesamtkunstwerk* with deceptive smoothness, despite Wagner's doubts that a symphonic poem with its programme must always leave aesthetic questions unanswered.[40] The composer's confidence in being able to follow Wagner directly surfaced unequivocally when his first opera *Guntram* was performed in 1894. In the poetic text, which the composer wrote himself, Strauss picked up Wagnerian images of a medieval brotherhood, while injecting new elements of Nietzschean subjectivity into the working out of his hero's fate. For although at the beginning of the opera the knight Guntram calls for revolution, he is later assailed by doubts and ends his life seeking his true self in solitude, like Nietzsche's vision in *Also sprach Zarathustra* of the prophet Zarathustra convalescing alone in his cave.

Strauss's revisions in *Guntram* of the view of cultural redemption associated with *Parsifal* or *Siegfried* were not welcomed in Bayreuth, despite the composer's plentiful references to Wagner's musical style. Indeed such revisions from within, even though applying insights from Wagner's own *Tristan*, were those most likely to be seen as dangerously insidious. In *Guntram* the hero insists on speaking for himself alone and departs from his knightly brotherhood: Strauss's subject-matter thus disturbs Wagner's delicate balance between the individual and the wider culture he seeks to represent, and the hero is shown using the Wagnerian style entirely as a vehicle for his own self-expression.

It may have been partly this sense of Strauss upsetting the smooth transference of Wagnerian values in *Guntram* – as well as its notorious technical difficulties – which caused his opera to be received so badly. Strauss's response in his following works, the symphonic poem *Till Eulenspiegel* and the opera *Feuersnot*, was to satirise the whole issue of the artist's place within his society or culture. In the symphonic poem, Till's motifs run riot through the various episodes which depict the scenes of his life; he remains the focus at every point, while the settings of the market or the judgement scene appear as simple backcloths for the expression of his personality. He thus cannot be described as a heroic figure; he does not truly engage with his external circumstances. His artistic self-expression shows itself to be both unfettered and unthreatening. Even *Feuersnot*, which is a more explicit tale of a young artist being isolated from his community for seeking to carry on his master's craft, betrays a sense of humorous artistic detachment. The story's crude symbolism of creative and sexual frustration is not allowed in any way to impede the development of a richly varied and satisfying Wagnerian orchestral texture. One is thus inclined to feel that the artist's hurt cannot be too serious, and that Strauss could have joined his powerful music to a more aspiring poetic text if he had wanted to. Strauss's symphonic poem *Ein Heldenleben* carries hints of a similarly perverse message. If the opening music depicts the artist as 'hero', as the programme claims, then his creative power is immediately obvious and the 'critics'' interruption of his symphonic flow is essentially self-inflicted. The eventual completion of the 'hero's' grandiose perfect cadence, interrupted at the end of the work's first section by the inconsequential whining of the 'critics', is never seriously in doubt; neither is the outcome of the struggle between the two parties in the later 'battle scene'. Strauss is essentially offering his audience an expression of unchallengeable heroism, a somewhat shocking prospect given his comparison of the work with Beethoven's *Eroica*. One might feel as if having watched Shakespeare's *Hamlet* Strauss dared to offer an easy cartoon version of the same story.

Contemporary audiences might have had some trouble distinguishing between the two versions of heroism; Romain Rolland describes how they would spring to their feet at performances of *Heldenleben* – 'the Germans have found their poet of Victory'.[41] Yet there is little doubt that Strauss himself was aware of the difference. It is assumed that he always intended the heroic figures in his works to portray aspects of his own personality; he certainly did much to reinforce such connections. However, his often ironic manipulation of the listener's responses makes one wonder whether there was not another 'artist-hero' working behind these images in *Heldenleben*, commenting through them to bring a subtler message. If so, then the message is never made explicit, nor is it made necessary to the immediate enjoyment of the work. One may see Strauss's multiple ironies either as one of the most effective post-Wagnerian strategies in defence of the self, or as a potentially cowardly retreat into silence.

The long-term appreciation of Strauss's artistic stance has certainly suffered from the willingness of audiences of the time to take most of his work entirely at face value. Arthur Seidl for one held Strauss up as the paradigmatic man of progress, success-fully extending Wagner's technical innovations in immediate matters of harmonic and orchestral colour and melodic line. And provided one did not pay too much atten-tion to the context in which Strauss placed such innovations, then one might imagine that he was still advocating the Bayreuth path – the steady and unquestioned exten-sion of Wagner's musical style. The unavoidable shock for audiences came with *Salome*, the opera which followed *Feuersnot*, for even the most spiritually short-sighted could not fail to notice that an eloquent extension of the language of Isolde's 'Liebestod' had now somehow become caught up in a nightmare of severed heads and obsessive lust. It was as though having flirted with images of himself as Wagner's successor, Strauss now accepted the full impact of Nietzsche's warnings against the contaminating influence of Wagner's style and opted for a much more radical denial of Wagner's world-view. For in *Salome* quasi-Wagnerian love music is unequivocally identified with sickness and decadence, and with false emotional fulfilment.

The message of *Salome* remains intact even in the far softer emotional climate of Strauss's later opera *Der Rosenkavalier*, as Octavian and the Marschallin make indul-gent and overblown references to Tristan and Isolde's love music in the opera's opening scene. Such exaggerated musical dialogue is shown to evaporate in the light of day and when faced by Baron Ochs's earthy view of sensuality. In the lyrical trio at the climax of the opera, the language of Wagnerian passion is frozen into song-like strophes and dramatically consigned to the past, while the future belongs to the folk-like simplicity of Octavian and Sophie's duet. It is difficult not to associate this final trio with the composer's own relinquishing of Wagnerian illusions. For though his following operas rekindled aspects of the Wagnerian style, they continued to be identified dramatically with a mood of lyrical nostalgia, and with ideas of dream or wish-fulfilment.

As with Mahler, the final outcome of Strauss's work adds many ironies to the label 'secessionist'; his revolutionary steps forward brought him back to a lyrical contemplation of the Wagnerian style, though now recognised as belonging to the past. Nietzsche himself doubted whether there were actually any positive stylistic alternatives to the Wagnerian sickness; all that was left to composers perhaps were various kinds of denial. He later admitted that his advocacy of Bizet's *Carmen* in *The Case of Wagner*, holding it out as the evocation of an entirely different musical style and spirit, was not meant to be taken as a realistic alternative to Wagnerian music drama, but more as a polemical gesture. Nietzsche confessed that, for him, 'Wagner sums up modernity. There is no way out, one must first become a Wagnerian.'[42]

Nietzsche in fact typifies the extreme reactions often provoked by Wagner's influence: swinging from complete partisanship to complete rejection – both in a sense recognising the power of Wagner's claims and both leaving much of his cultural diagnosis unchallenged. For although Nietzsche inveighed against the deception practised by Wagner, 'the *lie* of the great style',[43] he never actually showed directly how the lie might be countered and the elements of the musical language reassembled to create 'truth'.

Nietzsche's assumption was that a composer was powerless once he came too near to Wagner, a suggestion reinforced by both Mahler's and Strauss's tactics of separation. Their tactics certainly brought them success in the big public genres of the opera and symphony. They could not lightly be accused of artistic escapism, or of retiring into musical miniatures like the song-composer Hugo Wolf. One might say indeed that Wolf with his songs had chosen the easiest medium for winning any struggle for musical integrity – in Nietzsche's words:

> What can be done well today, what can be masterly, is only what is small. Here alone integrity is still possible.[44]

In the Lied the composer was not expected to make a public statement or speak for a wider culture, all was avowedly intimate and personal. Yet there was also the possibility of objectivity, for the composer was in one sense following the lead of the poet and thus could distance himself from the musical language of the song. Strauss's multiple ironies were here acknowledged aspects of the genre, to be exploited without raising constant reflections upon the stance of the composer himself. Wolf could offer himself inconspicuously as a seemingly neutral observer of the scene, picking up different aspects of Wagner's style and its poetic associations and exploring them for the course of a single song before moving on to others.

Within the Lied, the demands of personal authorship for stylistic and aesthetic consistency could be set against the given nature of the genre in a more precise way than in symphony or opera, and Wolf made a point of emphasising the attention due to the poet and to the formal limits of song. Thus Wolf was able to offer his listeners the contradictions of simple folk-like songs with Wagnerian undertones, or extremes of Wagnerian chromaticism in finely shaped and closed formal structures – a seemingly endless variety of formal and stylistic mixtures. Hans von Wolzogen confessed himself quite bewildered in his 1889 review of the *Mörike Lieder*, Wolf's first mature songbook. He tried to describe for his readers how Wolf could switch from:

> the cheerfully teasing, simple robust tunes of German folksong . . . to the strains of the Romantic ballad, full of ghostly horrors and elfish apparitions . . . up to the heights of hymn . . . and into the depths of mysticism.

He likened the experience of Wolf's music to being in a small boat, driven by impetuous waves; yet he believed one must trust the boat for it led to Mörike.[45] Wolzogen even recommended that Wolf's songs be performed alongside sections from Wagner's music dramas in the Wagner Societies. He only betrayed reservations when he realised the enthusiasm for Wolf as the 'new Schubert' as well as 'Wagner of the Lied' was in danger of placing him too high in the listeners' popularity.[46] Yet Wolzogen's temporary endorsement of Wolf was perhaps the nearest Bayreuth came to finding a follower who remained close to Wagner while exerting a healthy independence, so that his songs could appeal to Wagnerians and non-Wagnerians alike.

Wolf's success then as now was usually accredited to his happy choice of genre, allowing him, as in popular images of Schubert, to seem to sleepwalk his way through the complexities of the musical culture surrounding him. However, such images belie the gargantuan struggle which actually attended Wolf's relation to Wagner and the Wagnerians. As we shall see, while remaining financially and socially dependent on Wagnerian circles in Vienna, Wolf experienced his own Nietzschean battle, struggling to come to grips in his own way with the mixture of illusion and reality in Wagner's music dramas. Much of this could not be admitted openly for fear of his losing the Wagnerians' artistic support, but he continued to explore aspects of the question through the various songbooks, from the Mörike volume to the Michelangelo songs. And this was the way in which Wolf's relation to the Wagnerian inheritance differed most strongly from Mahler's and Strauss's. For unlike them he worked directly with the details of Wagner's style, exploring his language of illusion and reconsidering it within more definite tonal frames. As will be seen, the resulting twists and turns of musical expectation within a song provided Wolf with one of his most powerful poetic resources; as Wolzogen said, Wolf used musical surprises to lead his listener to the poet. However, his explorations also represented some of the most potent criticisms of Wagner's music and the claims made for it.

It was crucial to Wolf's achievements that he had his own access to the Classical tradition that Wagner had sought to appropriate, and this grounding he certainly gained from song. But the image of neutrality that he assumed by working through the Lied should not mask the significance of his critical achievements. Songs are as much an artistic statement as symphonies and operas, though Wolf had to fight hard for this to be recognised; and Wolf's songs can be interpreted as vital fuel for his Wagnerian critique, which in turn was the means for his renewal of the Lied. Wolf's importance as a Wagnerian critic should not indeed be underestimated, for the history of the Wagnerian inheritance suggests that a critic from within is precisely what was most needed. Only by composers facing out the prospect of stylistic contamination, as Nietzsche would have it, and recognising any illusions at their musical source could Wagner's legacy begin to be seen in complete perspective, open for reclaiming and reworking in as many ways as possible.

Chapter two

'Wagner of the Lied'? Wolf as critic of Wagner and Wagnerism

— ❦ —

When Wolf first made his impact as a writer on circles in Vienna in the 1880s it was as an eccentric music critic for the Sunday newspaper *Wiener Salonblatt*. It was not exactly the impact he would have wished for; Brahms recounts how he would wait for each issue of the paper with relish to see what lunacies the young man would come up with next.[1] Wolf's overly enthusiastic forays into the war of words between Brahms and Wagner supporters seemed ridiculous, particularly since they appeared in the pages of a journal for titbits and trivia. But Wolf's eyes were on a larger cause than the sale of popular newspapers – he was seeking to serve the cause of Wagnerism and Hugo Wolf. The two had become closely associated in his mind during his first years in Vienna a decade earlier, his need for self-promotion fanning his early Wagnerian enthusiasm into something bordering on fanaticism. When Wagner visited Vienna in 1875, Wolf ran after his coach wherever it went and stood in the lobby of Wagner's hotel until he was allowed to show the master some of his compositions.

Wolf's initial Wagnerian enthusiasm was the more remarkable since he then knew little of the music dramas themselves. As Wolf himself said: 'I conceived an irresistible inclination towards Richard Wagner, without having yet formed any conception of his music.' It was his reputation as the 'great Master of Tone . . . according to present opinion, the greatest opera composer of all' which attracted Wolf even before he heard *Tannhäuser* and *Lohengrin* a few days later.[2] Wolf described in letters to his parents all the trappings of Wagner's success – making him seem like a king coming to claim his rightful throne – pointing to them as evidence of what a musician could achieve in the world. Six months earlier Wolf had been almost persuaded to give up his own musical career altogether, 'since I see that a musician is a wholly contemptible person in your eyes'.[3] Now he felt he could present his parents with a new and different vision of a musician's worth, one which remained with Wolf as the measure for his own efforts. For in later life the composer was always making outsize claims for his music, whether in comparing a relatively slight song such as *Der Jäger* with *Tristan und Isolde,*[4] or declaring that his opera *Der Corregidor* would demolish the works of Italian *verismo* and German fairy-tale opera at one stroke.[5]

The Oedipal conflict which is often seen as motivating an artist's endeavour was transparently evident from the beginning of Wolf's dealings with Wagner. After a performance of *Götterdämmerung* he was found in tears, inveighing against the bitter fate which had made him a musician after such a composer and saying: 'One thing I can do which Wagner was not able to – starve!'[6] Yet interestingly enough it is not love for Wagner's music but for Schumann's that first turned Wolf into a composer. Susan Youens has recently shown the extent to which Wolf served out his song apprenticeship from 1876 'under the sign of Schumann', returning again and again to the texts of Heine, the poet most associated with Schumann, and then having to struggle to rid himself of stylistic resemblances that were too close.[7] By contrast Wolf did not refer to Wagner's style until the Mörike songbook of 1888, thirteen years after first hearing Wagner's music, at a stage when his approach to song-writing had passed beyond apprenticeship to full maturity. Thus while the composer's response to Schumann seemed like an involuntary possession, his relationship with Wagner followed a different pattern. As will be seen later, in the Mörike songs Wolf laid out different aspects of Wagner's style in a quite systematic fashion, moulding and directing them to create distinctive and unexpected results. Here Wolf can be seen to use references to Wagnerian features as part of a conscious act of criticism and self-definition, a declaration of artistic power and independence.

However, Wolf must have known that there was little chance that the Mörike songs would be recognised as such an achievement by the public. Song was seen as being a dependent genre by its very nature, relying on associations with the past, with poetry or with other genres to achieve its artistic significance. Certainly a composer would not be able to make his living from just writing songs, unless perhaps he were prepared to lower his sights and pander to the tastes of the domestic or salon market. If he wished to succeed with the wider concert-going public then he needed to borrow from the genres of symphony or opera. So one finds Wolf, like many other song composers of the time, engaged in expanding his songs into orchestral or choral versions, ready to attract the notice of a wider audience and to gain prestige for himself.[8] One also sees him persisting in his lifelong ambition to write opera, to challenge Wagner on his own territory.

Thus Wolf found himself embroiled in conflicts with Wagner and Wagnerism not in the sense of fighting for an inner identity, but through the circumstance of feeling he needed to adopt the outer mantle of Wagner for artistic prestige. Once, when he had uttered a particularly rude remark about Wagner to his friend Emil Kauffmann, Wolf came near to admitting that he lived a kind of double life:

> Wagner's excesses degrade one into a worm. However you must not think that I have suddenly joined the anti-Wagnerians, an event which I have earnestly to guard against, if only to justify my own artistic existence.[9]

The strains of keeping to any kind of Wagnerian identity became obvious later in Wolf's career, but even in the early years of the *Salonblatt* criticisms, 1884 to 1887, there were signs that he was acting a part. His notorious reviews of Brahms's music were the most obvious examples of inflated partisanship. Wolf was later ashamed of his imaginative excesses and even admitted to his friend Edmund Hellmer that he liked some of Brahms's works.[10] One suspects that he was adversely affected in his reviewing by Brahms's severe comments on his own early songs when the young composer visited him in 1879. One year previously, Wolf had been enthusiastic about attending a performance of Brahms's First Symphony and had also approached Hanslick, the most powerful of Brahms's supporters, for an opinion of his music. Even after the fateful visit of 1879 Wolf followed up some of Brahms's and Hanslick's suggestions, enquiring about the possibility of lessons with Nottebohm and of having his work published by Simrock. Both of these projects failed, and it may have been the sense that all doors to the Brahms circle were shut which encouraged Wolf to throw in his lot so publicly with the Wagnerians. Certainly once the reviews from the *Salonblatt* began to emerge, with their lampoons of Brahms as a composer of a 'dead-tired fantasy [running] the gauntlet between "can't do" and "wish I could"',[11] Wolf was treated as a 'non-person' by the established music critics of Vienna.[12] The Rosé Quartet refused to perform his D minor string quartet in 1885, and in 1886 Hans Richter subjected the composer to a most humiliating scene when he conducted a public play-through of his symphonic poem *Penthesilea*. Richter made no efforts to control the orchestra as it mangled the difficult score; in the midst of the cacophony he said loudly enough for all to hear – 'and this is the man who dares to criticise Brahms!'[13] From this time on it became clear that the Viennese Wagner Society would be the only reliable venue for Wolf's work. Heinrich Werner, Wolf's close friend, described how the Wagnerians believed that the young composer was suffering from the critics on Wagner's behalf and therefore deserved their support.[14] From 1887 the tenor Ferdinand Jäger, a famous Siegfried in the past, began to perform Wolf's songs regularly in the 'internal evenings' of the Society, and Josef Schalk embarked on a series of critical articles, the first, 'Neue Lieder, neues Leben', appearing in 1890 and bringing Wolf a wider following from beyond Vienna.[15]

As in their dealings with Bruckner, the Wagnerians succeeded in subverting the effect of the ban from the Viennese establishment and offered Wolf some kind of public. However, there is little sign that he was satisfied with their efforts. Werner confirms that the Viennese Wagner Society acted as a Hugo Wolf Society in as much as was compatible with its nature.[16] Gustav Schur, the Wagner Society's treasurer, describes organising a fund for Wolf's support even though this created problems with the Society's statutes.[17] And yet Wolf remained cool or even hostile towards the Society. As Schur wrote:

> In [Wolf's] opinion the Society did not offer him what he felt he had the right to demand from his friends. Namely, the unconditional single-minded devotion to him and his work.[18]

Wolf did not accept that he should be identified as Wagner's product and supported for his sake,[19] or that everything should always be seen through the master's eyes. As he once complained of the Wagner Societies,

> Anything that is not tied up with an umbilical chord to Wagner does not exist for them and anyone who wants to loose himself from it is decried as an apostate.[20]

Clearly the partisanship of Wolf's early reviews had placed him in a false position, creating a dangerous split between his role as Wagnerian disciple and his irrepressible desire for critical independence. Even in the *Salonblatt* reviews the latter manifested itself, sometimes in unexpected ways. For example his judgements on performance drew on standards other than Wagner's one of being true to the demands of a poetic text or of emotional expression. He would sometimes refer to absolute musical boundaries in a way which seemed to owe more to Hanslick's ideas of the 'purely musical':

> Is art served, or can the public find refreshment when, for example, cellist X seeks effects on his instrument appropriate to the piccolo, or when violinist Y tries to imitate on his E string the rough voice of the double bass, or when a contralto reaches for the high C and a soprano for the low G, not to speak of pianists? Things can hardly be madder in a lunatic asylum than in a concert hall.[21]

Wolf had a definite sense of what was appropriate to an instrument or a genre and would not allow that these might be forgotten, even in moments of Wagnerian exultation. 'Exultation' was a state much prized by Wolf. According to Ernest Newman he once said: 'The true test of a composer is this, – *can he exult?* Wagner can exult; Brahms cannot.'[22] However, he also warned singers that they should discriminate between 'projecting passions' and 'being passionate' if they wished to avoid a coarsely exaggerated performance.[23] In Wolf's opinion seeking the effect of exultation was no excuse for lack of artistic control. Elsewhere he advised a song-writer that he must always compose in 'cool blood' if he were to succeed in setting down his excited feelings.[24] He did not approve of people confusing the experiences of the man with the artist, and unlike Wagner endeavoured to keep the two images of himself separate in other people's minds.[25]

The full implications of these shifts away from Wagnerian thinking were only realised in Wolf's letters and comments from 1890 onwards and in his practice in the songs themselves. However, the *Salonblatt* reviews confirm that the roots were there from 1884, so that later disagreements with the Wagnerians cannot be seen as merely brought on by pique at his not receiving the attention he felt he deserved. Werner once suggested that Wolf's remarks about Wagner's music degrading one into a worm were 'just the expression of momentary outbursts', a sign that even before the onset of his madness in 1897 Wolf suffered bouts of mental instability.[26] But again the evidence points to a more serious and considered criticism on Wolf's part. The composer's most significant 'outburst' occurred in 1889 when some students used a performance of his song *Heimweh* (Homesickness) to mount a nationalistic demonstration. As they three times interrupted the song's closing bars with loud applause, Wolf stormed out of the Wagner Society declaring he would never come back. In his subsequent letter to Josef Schalk he argued through the reasons for his departure and said the rewards of publicity could not compensate him for the conflicts and trials he experienced in the Society:

> The devil of vanity and inordinate ambition will not catch me by the forelock again, you can depend on that. I am no senseless Mohammed to propagate my things with fire and sword, and none of my friends shall lose a single hair on my account. Let each seek to win through on his own account; each one has enough to do to look after himself. So let's have no more apostles![27]

In this letter Wolf rejected not only the Society but also Schalk's role as mediator with all the compromises it brought in its wake. He was persuaded to return a month later, but the protective wall which according to Werner Schalk had built around the composer had shown its frailty and the relationship between them grew much less close. Wolf still respected Schalk, still turning to him for criticism of his work at various points in his later life, but any remnant of Schalk's vision of the Wagner Society as an enlightened artistic brotherhood had dissolved in the composer's eyes under the experience of 'being made the object of the silliest judgments from sundry unwashed mouths'.[28]

After 1889 Wolf did not quite live up to his resolution of renouncing publicity altogether, of composing as a private individual. But he did begin to seek a different public identity, one distinct from Wagner and the Wagnerians. The cry 'so let's have no more apostles!' as well as Wolf's disparaging remarks on the worthlessness of popularity reveal the growing influence of Nietzsche upon the composer. He would often quote the philosopher's aphorisms, for example 'I listened for an echo and only heard praise'[29] and 'Praise is more troublesome than blame.'[30] Some knowledge of Nietzsche might be taken for granted in Viennese Wagnerian circles. In his early days Wolf was a regular visitor to the famous Café Griensteidl, where Wagner's writings would be discussed alongside Nietzsche's *The Birth of Tragedy, Human, All too Human* and *Untimely Meditations*.[31] However the appearance of *The Case of Wagner* in 1888 had an unusually profound effect upon the composer; according to his friend Friedrich Eckstein it threw him into complete mental turmoil.[32] While he rejected Nietzsche's extreme criticisms of Wagner's music, he felt irresistibly drawn by many of his other opinions and by his manner of expressing them. The philosopher's enthusiastic championship of *Carmen* found an echo in Wolf's own admiration for Bizet. He also shared Nietzsche's passion for Chopin, one which had embroiled him in many arguments with Schalk and others of the Wagner Society for whom Chopin remained 'undeutsch' and a 'Salonmusiker'. Like Nietzsche Wolf gloried in Chopin's 'aristocratic refinement', seeing such qualities reflected in the philosopher's own prose style. According to Eckstein, the 'glitzernd-leuchtende Sprache' (radiantly glittering language) of *The Case of Wagner* almost cast a spell on

Wolf;[33] he would later describe Wagner's language by contrast as 'long-winded and tapeworm-like'.[34]

Nietzsche's manner of expression remained an inspiration to Wolf even if he continued to doubt aspects of his musical judgement. Eckstein recounts how Wolf insisted on identifying the composer who the philosopher thought was the only person capable of writing an overture 'all in one piece' and deserving to be placed above Wagner. When Eckstein eventually traced the reference to Peter Gast's *Der Löwe von Venedig*, Wolf asked him how on earth one could make sense of the philosopher's idolisation of such a worthless piece of music.[35] If Wolf had known Nietzsche's own music he would probably have doubted the quality of his musical taste and understanding even more. However, far from undermining Nietzsche's appeal, his uncertain musical credentials left Wolf free to apply the philosophy in his own fashion without feeling the need to relinquish anything of his musical leadership to the philosopher. Thus although Wolf often came near to quoting *The Case of Wagner* as he described the kind of opera he wished to write, he was very far from finding an actual blueprint there for his new style of comic opera. Like Nietzsche, Wolf believed in a Mediterranean atmosphere of 'strumming guitars, sighs of love, moonlit nights, champagne carousals' as a healthy antidote to Wagnerian music drama and an escape from the 'sombre world-redeeming spectre of a Schopenhauerian philosophy in the background'.[36] Yet the actual artistic means Wolf employed in setting up his alternative view of opera were very much home-grown and owed little to Bizet's *Carmen* or any other operatic model.

Der Corregidor, Wolf's setting of Alarcon's novel *El Sombrero de tres Picos*, finally appeared in 1896, but he had been planning a Spanish comic opera since 1882.[37] Even with the composition of the Mörike songs the composer was wondering to his friends whether a comic opera might not be about to emerge, and at the time of the Spanish songbook in 1889 he was specifically concerned with thoughts of the Alarcon novel. Two of the Spanish songs were eventually incorporated into *Der Corregidor* and a further two were planned for inclusion in *Manuel Venegas*, Wolf's setting of Alarcon's *El Niño de la Bola*, left unfinished at his death. Thus Wolf harboured plans for an alternative kind of opera well before he read *The Case of Wagner*, and continued to explore aspects of his ideas in his songs while searching for a suitable libretto. For a while none of the librettos offered, including the Rosa Mayreder text which he eventually used for *Der Corregidor*, seemed to Wolf worthy of his intentions. His operatic ambitions and plans were in danger of dwindling away – fuelled by dissatisfaction with Wagner and encouraged by identification with Nietzsche, but incapable of realisation.

One can readily understand how as the years passed the wish to write an opera became for Wolf a test of his credibility as a composer. His decision in 1895 to return to the rejected Mayreder libretto, after four years of artistic stagnation, seems like an act of desperation – a conscious decision to avoid further prevarication and plunge into composition as though the problems of matching text to music did not exist. The end result reveals that the problems were far from solved; Mayreder failed to simplify the detailed action of Alarcon's novel and to create the slower dramatic pacing required for musical setting. Often ignoring the need for an overall shape or direction, Wolf tended to approach each parcel of text as its own entity, so creating a musical patchwork of disjointed scenes and small bursts of action.

As an opera *Der Corregidor* is desperately flawed, yet, taken as it is, it still offers a fascinating insight into the nature of Wolf's musical and dramatic instincts, and their often distinctly anti-Wagnerian bias. It also offers a most unusual view of human character and its relation to dramatic narrative, showing Wolf questioning the basic Romantic supposition that character controls destiny. For in *Der Corregidor* Wolf does not sustain consistent dramatic personalities across the piecemeal arrangement of scenes. Instead he allows his characterisations to shift with each new situation, to create, intentionally or unintentionally, an almost impersonal play of circumstances. Indeed, with the composer giving his attention to adapting song frameworks to a broader flow of action, he creates a new emphasis upon dramatic context which can be seen to have psychological ramifications well beyond immediate questions of style and technique.

As one might expect, as a compositional starting-point Wolf grasped every possible opportunity in the libretto for an occasional song, any occasion when one might suppose a character to be literally singing, whether the Nightwatchman calling the hours, Frasquita singing at her spinning-wheel or entertaining a guest, or the Corregidor singing to cheer himself up; for these last two situations Wolf even managed to incorporate two of the songs from his Spanish songbook, *In dem Schatten meiner Locken* and *Herz, verzage nicht geschwind*. From his letters it is clear that Wolf began his composition of the opera at one such obvious point, Tio Lukas's drinking-song in Act II scene 8. Wolf must have considered this 'song' a good entry into the dramatic action of the opera, since with this music the hero Lukas tricks his captors, the Corregidor's henchmen, into thinking he is drunk so that he can escape back to his wife Frasquita and protect her from the Corregidor's wiles. The sense of confusion about where the drinking-song begins and ends is thus a good depiction of drunkenness, as well as an example of how to adapt the closed structures of song to a more open dramatic pacing.

The opera is indeed full of attempted extensions and links, to the extent that it is often hard to distinguish the important musical landmarks from the smaller-scale signposts. Even when one extended song-structure seems to have been superseded by some new material, Wolf often links this back into the previous framework, so that it is revealed as simply another extension. Thus in Act I scene 4 the material of Frasquita's 'song' to entertain the Corregidor *In dem Schatten* spreads its tentacles far beyond the original song. In its unextended state the Lied already makes much play of shifting tonal and rhythmic perspectives, as the singer mocks her bemused lover. The orchestra is given a prominent motif, a Spanish *fandango* figure, which sometimes helps outline a clear four-bar phrasing and sometimes is extended into ostinato

Example 2.1   Wolf, *Der Corregidor*, Act I scene 4

patterns of indefinite length. The balancing pauses – as with the words 'Weck' ich ihn nun auf?' (Shall I wake him?) – suggest a reassuring rhythmic containment, matching the poetic image of the lover sleeping in the woman's arms. But these pauses are often linked to harmonic sequences of rising thirds, suggesting such peace might be illusory and the singer should not be trusted (see Example 2.1).[38] One of the joys of the song is that one cannot ever quite distinguish between the woman's mood of loving concern and mockery, the fluctuations of motivic rhythm and phrasing are so subtle. In the song, taken by itself, the precise close renders further answers unnecessary. The emotional ambiguity has been fully captured through Wolf's refinement of the motivic material, just as the poem uses the image of the woman's hair to blend inextricably ideas of loving protection with those of deadly entanglement.

In the opera the questions of motivation surrounding *In dem Schatten* cannot be so easily dismissed, and as the Corregidor joins Frasquita and adds to her closing phrase, the boundaries between the song and the circumstances in which she sings it become blurred. The Corregidor clearly wishes to believe that the 'sleeping lover' of the song can be identified with Frasquita's husband Lukas, dozing in the arbour above them, and he hopes that in singing so mockingly of Lukas Frasquita is now ready to try her seductive powers elsewhere. He whispers his further conclusion in the direct style of *In dem Schatten* – 'Lass ihn schlafen, lass ihn ruhn' (Let him sleep, let him rest) – and then hastens to introduce his own contrasting material whose passionate mood cannot be in doubt (see Example 2.2).

However, the Corregidor's bid to exert control over the scene is soon undermined by seeping returns to the *fandango* rhythms of Example 2.1. One might say that the Corregidor, having blurred the boundaries of Frasquita's song, had played into her hands, allowing the tone of ironic dialogue to continue and spill over into his own efforts at love-making. Even in his first passionate outburst of Example 2.2, the

Example 2.2   Wolf, *Der Corregidor*, Act I scene 4

Corregidor.

Example 2.3   Wolf, *Der Corregidor*, Act I scene 4

orchestral phrasing marks out clear two- and four-bar divisions to underpin the singer's declamatory flight. As his eloquence is tested, the orchestral punctuation becomes more pronounced, finally emerging in a fully-fledged ostinato motif (see Example 2.3). The rising mediant shifts every two bars and the teasing chromatic slides of Example 2.3 help point an ironic reference back to Example 2.1's motivic rhythms. Frasquita is here asking the Corregidor to find an appointment for her nephew in return for her love, and it is clear she is teasing him, just as the speaker of *In dem Schatten* teased her sleeping lover.

A simple analysis of Wolf's musico-dramatic strategy in this scene would be that he wishes to show Frasquita wielding a stylistic and formal power through song, while the Corregidor helplessly attempts a more open-ended discourse. His love-making and his magisterial authority lead him nowhere, despite their immediate impressiveness. However, looked at in the broader context for this interaction, Frasquita cannot be credited with taking a particular initiative when singing *In dem Schatten*. The song is woven into the general fabric of the opera by another set-piece, an introductory

Example 2.4   Wolf, *Der Corregidor*, Act I scene 3

dance which directly anticipates the *fandango* rhythms and tonal and harmonic character of the song to follow. And this dance is preceded in its turn by a set-piece 'song'
from Repela, the Corregidor's pretentious servant. Unusually in the opera, this 'song'
is not extended; it is the most obviously closed scene of the opera. The self-contained
eight-bar introduction is repeated four times as part of a definite ternary structure,
even though Repela apes his master's wandering declamatory phrasing and engages
in conversational dialogue with Frasquita. His exaggerated rhyming cadences appear
strikingly mannered and self-conscious (see Example 2.4).

Every time Repela appears in the opera he is accompanied by similarly exaggerated
song styles, casting an ironic light on all around him, Frasquita included. In Act III
scene 2, when Frasquita is fleeing from the Corregidor through the dark, she stumbles
upon Repela and ends up singing a tripping duet with him, which can only seem
bizarre in such circumstances. Yet it becomes clear from looking at Repela's role as a
whole that his use of song styles is not actually a display of his power or control over
others, but rather a recognition of the game they are all involved in, whether they like
it or not. Wolf's friends disliked the cynicism that emanated from this servant and
advised the composer to cut him out of the opera altogether. But Wolf replied that
Repela was his favourite character; not that he gave him a moral superiority over the
faithful and sorely tested husband and wife, Lukas and Frasquita, but that he represented a clear-sightedness nearest to Wolf's own in his efforts at dramatic characterisation.

For in refusing to take up in *Der Corregidor* a transcendent view of character as
inherent in Wagnerian music drama, Wolf let all the human frailties and ambiguities
appear, even in his 'hero' Lukas. It is highly significant that Lukas is first presented, in
Act I scene 1, in interaction with a neighbour, one whom Wolf described as summing
up all that was small-minded in human society.[39] The ostinato motif which dominates the first scene comes later to be identified as Lukas's own, but, unlike a

Example 2.5 Wolf, *Der Corregidor*, Act I scene 1

Example 2.6 Wolf, *Der Corregidor*, Act I scene 2

Wagnerian leitmotif, it makes no immediate impact. It functions as a simple building-block in the song-framework, much like the *fandango* figure in Example 2.1 (see Example 2.5). When a varied version of this repeated figure returns at the end of Act I scene 2 the 'Lukas motif' is replaced by the 'Corregidor motif', without much change being registered (see Example 2.6).[40] The essential neutrality of both these motifs is striking, even though the characters associated with them are of highly contrasting moral status. In Act I scene 1 Lukas is not distinguished in tone from his envious neighbour; he falls in with the balanced phrases and ternary structure, obvious formal patterns which are rounded off with a simple and dismissive close.

As Frasquita enters at the beginning of scene 2, one might imagine that she would take the level of conversation in the opera to a new intensity. The rhythmic building-blocks from scene 1 are extended into a new song-framework. But this is a 'song' to

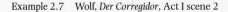

Example 2.7   Wolf, *Der Corregidor*, Act I scene 2

Example 2.8   Wolf, *Der Corregidor*, Act I scene 2

invite imaginary guests to the mill to taste their wine, rather than a love-song to Lukas, and it is as though the envious neighbour were still present in spirit. Indeed the rhythmic patterns of Example 2.5 can be seen reflected in Example 2.7, even if more melodically presented (see Example 2.7). Lukas begins to stretch the vocabulary of the musical dialogue with rhythmic and modulatory extensions, preparing for a passionate embrace with his wife at the climax of the scene. Yet the textural and registral expansion at this point does not prevent the rhythmic markings of Example 2.5 and Example 2.7 from still being apparent (see Example 2.8). And in fact this scene closes soon afterwards in the exact manner of scene 1, so that the two phases of the action are effectively superimposed; one has the sense that the characters are still engaged in going through the formalities with each other, in a well-rehearsed game which always ends up following the same pattern.

It is against the background of these two scenes that Repela makes his entry in scene 3 and performs his exaggeratedly formal set-piece, as an ironic commentary on those around him. As already discussed, Frasquita uses song-patterns to draw obvious rings around the Corregidor. But Wolf has succeeded in raising an unsettling question about whether she is truly any more in control of the 'game' than the Corregidor himself. When at the climax of his attempted seduction in scene 4 the Corregidor falls off his stool, the orchestra steadies the previous rhythmic momentum with a further return to Example 2.5's building-blocks (see Example 2.9). And from this point, as might seem inevitable, this much extended scene is drawn back towards the same cheerfully inconsequential music that closed scenes 1 and 2.

Example 2.9 Wolf, *Der Corregidor*, Act I scene 4

Example 2.10 Wolf, *Der Corregidor*, Act II scene 1

Example 2.11 Wolf, *Der Corregidor*, Act II scene 1

In one sense it is dramatically reassuring that the Corregidor's flights of passion should be so easily resolved; it anticipates how his more violent attempts on Frasquita's virtue in Act II also come to nothing. However, such formal objectivity has its chilling aspect too, suggesting that Frasquita and Lukas's expressions of love in Act I scene 2 might also be lightly dismissed. Their love music in Act II scene 1 provides a rather welcome contrast. For though beginning with Example 2.5's style of punctuating figures, these soon lead into a new kind of lyricism, where the melodic arch diverts attention from the constant rhyming patterns (Example 2.10). With such emphasis upon the melodic moment, Wolf allows a new temporal space to invade the opera. When Example 2.10 is interrupted by the sound of knocking, it is not clear for once how the sectional patchwork of the opera will be resumed. 'Lukas's motif' is extended beyond its usual one-bar shape, into an ominous pause (see Example 2.11).

Example 2.12   Wolf, *Der Corregidor*, Act II scene 2

Example 2.13   Wolf, *Der Corregidor*, Act III scene 3

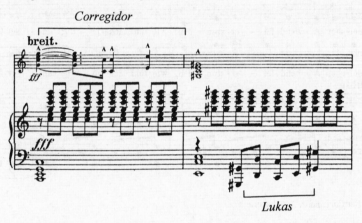

Once the Corregidor's drunken official Tonuelo enters, the inconsequential pattern of dialogue re-emerges and the tone of the opera closes in again (see Example 2.12). However, the suggestion now remains that there might be another perspective to the dramatic action, beyond Repela's cynicism. This perspective is addressed directly in the emotional crisis of the opera, Act III scene 3, where Lukas, having escaped from Tonuelo and his drunken crew, returns to his mill to see through the keyhole the Corregidor asleep in his own bed. Without realising that Frasquita has already safely fled the scene, he believes his world to be in ruins. Parts of previous exchanges come back to him, as disordered echoes and song-reminiscences lapsing, unusually, into silence. Example 2.11 dominates the opening of the scene. It is followed eventually by the more patterned figures of Example 2.9 and Example 2.3, but these too tail off into silence. It is only when these figures begin to be seen against the larger backdrop of the third and fourth scenes of Act III as a whole that a sense of direction emerges. For Example 2.11 appears three times in these scenes, creating a loose strophic structure. On its second appearance it is again followed by Example 2.9, and these two figures become joined together by a version of the 'Corregidor's motif' which expands to embrace both ideas (see Example 2.13).

Such a motivic statement as Example 2.13 might seem to overflow song-bound-

Example 2.14   Wolf, *Der Corregidor*, Act III scene 4

aries, suggesting that all the 'games' are finally over perhaps, and the Corregidor has won. However, once silence has again intervened, Example 2.11 is drawn into a further climactic statement – one which outstrips Example 2.13. The impressive motif which now appears is associated with the Corregidor's wife, Mercedes, and is conceived throughout the opera as a monumental block-like statement, similar in rhythmic simplicity to Example 2.13, though the harmonic textures suggest a more convincing sense of scale and forward momentum (see Example 2.14). These mediant-style progressions, while striking in themselves, direct forwards to the point of resolution in a new version of 'Lukas's motif' in a way that is decisive for the scene and the opera as a whole. The repetitive figures which spring up from the moment of cadence in bar 10 of Example 2.14 resume the opera's familiar rhythmic patterns, but they now have a newly defined function – filling in the larger structure of scenes 3 and 4 – rather than being part of an indefinite chain of song-extensions.

This pair of scenes in Act III is indeed the largest of the opera's dramatic structures. It is measured out in a deliberate fashion which exceeds the scale of the earlier conversational dialogues. Yet, as the manner of its rounding off confirms, this structure still holds to the styles and shape of song. Lukas cannot escape the 'games' set up by his fellows, nor in the end does he wish to; rather, he turns them to his own advantage. At the end of scene 4 he dons the Corregidor's clothes, in a spirit of farce as well as revenge. From this point the opera rushes towards its conclusion with no more moments of reflection upon the seriousness of the action or its consequences. But now the song-material has been stretched to its furthest point in Act III scenes 3 and 4, there is a greater sense of meaning in the patterns which follow. They reflect the assurance that comes from Lukas's discovery of an answer to the Corregidor's threats, in the person of his wife Mercedes. Her music, while being in some ways part of the 'game' observed by Repela, also marks its limit, the textural and harmonic extreme which pulls the material back to resolution and containment.

Mercedes's motif performs this function most clearly at the end of the opera where she leads in the final chorus of simple thanksgiving, all agreeing that thanks to her the various 'adventures' surrounding her husband have ended without harm. We might echo some of the bemusement of the Corregidor, who still wishes to know what exactly happened when Lukas entered Mercedes's bedroom to exact his revenge, and how all the threats and counter-threats have come to be resolved. Yet Mercedes is undoubtedly right to refuse any direct answers. The 'game', as portrayed by Wolf, has had its own momentum and cannot be easily summarised; it is enough that we can accept that it has come to an end. Much of the detail of the opera has to remain ambiguous in its quickly shifting moods, between mockery and passion.

In Wolf's songs such subtlety and ambiguity have always been greatly appreciated, but in *Der Corregidor* they created a huge barrier to the performance and reception of the work. Wolf refused to accept any restraint upon his imagination and to adapt to the slower, simpler pace of scenic action. Like Nietzsche, he despised the coarser gestures which were the usual vocabulary of the theatre. After the music of *Der Corregidor* was finished many of his friends were indeed dismayed by his lack of interest in the opera's theatrical presentation; Wolf said such things were the business of the librettist. Indeed the musical language of the opera was so detailed that the composer faced producers and performers with insurmountable problems. The singers at the first performance had great difficulty sustaining the vocal precision Wolf required, never mind the problems of timing their physical actions to the music.

Given such practical evidence one might believe that Wolf's vision of a radical alternative to Wagnerian music drama was indeed unrealisable. However, he did succeed in substantiating his criticism of Wagner in his opera, offering contrasts which could not be passed off among his contemporaries as resulting from the change of genre from music drama to song. Karl Heckel, a friend and publisher of Wolf's, pointed out how antipathetic the composer had proved to be to the 'powerful pathos' of Wagner's music.[41] In his opinion both Wolf and the librettist Rosa Mayreder – herself a well-known Nietzschean – echoed in *Der Corregidor* the philosopher's 'aristocratic contempt' for direct sentimental appeals to the public. Wolf was striving for the 'light step' Nietzsche so longed for from musicians, holding back the immediate expressive power of his music with a 'powerful and noble control of form'.[42]

Heckel was accused by some of exaggerating the composer's distance from Wagner in order to justify Wolf's refusal to set Heckel's own Wagnerian-style libretto.

However, another of Wolf's friends, Edmund Hellmer, also spoke in Nietzschean terms of the epigrammatic nature of Wolf's opera, his successful avoidance of all moral didacticism and his overriding objectivity:

> He doesn't stand in the middle of the mood and its emotion, he stands above it. This is why his music gives the impression of being absolute, pure, healthy. It is perhaps the 'Joyful Knowledge', the cheerful spirituality which Nietzsche demanded from music.[43]

Hellmer even suggested that *Der Corregidor* had suffered in performance because the German stage – under the sway of Wagner – was not yet free enough for such high-flying spirituality.[44]

Such remarks proved highly controversial among Wolf's supporters in the Wagner Society. Gustav Schur, along with many other Wagnerians, had supported the founding of a Viennese Hugo Wolf Society in 1897. He left in protest when these comments appeared at the head of a series of essays on *Der Corregidor* published by the Hugo Wolf Society in 1899.[45] The split was perhaps inevitable. The newly formed Wolf Society acknowledged the role which the Wagner Society had played but sought to distance itself from any Wagnerian propaganda. For example the singer Ferdinand Jäger was not invited to become a member despite having been so strongly associated with Wolf's music in the past. The new society felt the Wagnerian style of his performances failed to bring out the melodic qualities of the songs and distorted the public's view of them.[46]

The Wolf Society even felt it had to be distanced from the composer himself. His personality always attracted controversy and the society wished to allow the focus to fall upon his music, to let it speak for itself in all its subtlety. For in the view of Michael Haberlandt, the Wolf Society's chairman, Wolf's music never imposed itself on an audience in 'flashy effects'. In its 'deep inwardness it holds back like Cordelia and scorns to speak in the open market-place'.[47] Here was a kind of admission that Wolf's music had been steam-rollered by a cause not its own and a plea to listen with a new attentiveness. Yet the comparisons with Cordelia are perhaps a little overdone. In song, as in opera, Wolf was quite prepared to challenge any Wagnerian assumptions openly as well as subtly. And although the genre of the Lied was not always considered of the greatest critical significance at the time, with hindsight one can see that attitudes to song actually played a highly important role in the make-up of Wagnerian music drama and its influence. Thus far from shying away from the mainstream of musical ideas as some have thought, Wolf continued to place himself at the centre, eventually revealing song as a most fertile battleground for a critic of Wagner like himself.

Chapter three

Small things can also enchant us – Wolf's challenge to nineteenth-century views of song

※

On the evidence of Wolf's life there are many signs that he struggled with the image of himself as a specialist song-writer, sensing the limitations this placed on him in the eyes of the public. He once said that he even regretted the popularity his songs received because it implied he was incapable of composing anything larger.[1] He wished to assert himself more unmistakably in the genre of opera, but he also believed that his songs were of the greatest artistic significance if only people would recognise it. The composer would inveigh against concert organisers bypassing his 'small things' in favour of 'greater riches',[2] believing that like Josef Schalk – who created a furor by performing Wolf's songs with Beethoven orchestral music in one of the Viennese Wagner Society's concerts – they should be prepared to go against the tide of common opinion. Indeed several critics joined Wolf in warning audiences, composers and performers of the dangers of valuing musical size and stylistic effect over subtler matters of spiritual content. Max Graf, for one, believed that it was 'psychological effects, unseen affinities, which more than any other aesthetic values, should identify an artist as modern'.[3] The philosopher Friedrich Hausegger also encouraged composers to follow an aesthetic of 'inwardness', as summed up in his idea of 'Musik als Ausdruck' (Music as expression).[4] However, the clearest lead came from Nietzsche, with his claim that integrity was now only possible in what was small – an opinion which must have encouraged Wolf as he developed a more and more pronounced miniaturism in his songs.

The title of the opening number of Wolf's last major songbook, the Italian songs – *Auch kleine Dinge können uns entzücken* (Small things can also enchant us) – certainly reads like a declaration of artistic intent. Many of the Paul Heyse translations of anonymous Italian folk-poems which Wolf chose to set here are notable for their concern with various aspects of 'smallness'. Thus the composer selected those poems which conform to the restricted six or eight-line structure of the popular Italian *rispetto*, offering a personal view of life through the expression of a single poetic idea or conceit. The ideas themselves are also often not profound but 'small' in scope, arising from the circumstances of everyday life as felt by ordinary people. Any intensity comes from the almost obsessive focus upon a particular detail, the observation of something small which then becomes the carrier of feeling, whether a detail of the beloved's appearance – her hair, her glance, her proud walk – or a detail of conversation or behaviour.

The narrowness of the Italian poems' emotional content has made some people question why Wolf chose to set these texts at all. The contrast between them and the greater psychological depth of the better-known Mörike or Goethe songs, or even the Spanish songs, is certainly striking. However if Wolf's concern was indeed to reveal the beauty and power hidden in 'small things', then his choice of the Italian poems makes complete sense. Even the overlapping of the composition of these songs with the opera *Der Corregidor* fits into a clear artistic intention. For as already discussed, in the opera Wolf chose to avoid the development of an expansive emotional content, instead using song-structures to control and hold back the emotional temperature of the work. In the opera Wolf's ironic impulse to stand outside the drama and pathos of a scene and to hold them within small-scale patterns was certainly taken to unexpected lengths. And in the Italian songs the same uncompromising view of time was at work. The sense of close-working symmetries directing and controlling the musical expression is present throughout each song. Thus at the beginning of *Auch kleine Dinge*, decorative semiquavers in the piano prelude circle around single pitches, pitches which the lower part resolves into triadic configurations surrounding the tonic A (see Example 3.1). The sense of pattern expands from the single beat, to the harmonic pull of the one-bar and then two-bar units. Once the four-bar unit is outlined with chromatic movements towards bar 5 and the arrival on A major at the entry of the voice, the enclosing shape of the song is fully established. Each subsequent four-bar phrase retraces the arrival back on A; the descending scale in the bass, moving in parallel thirds with the right hand's semiquavers, reinforces the continuing pull to the tonic.

The sense of imminent closure in this song is far more literal than in any of the scenes from *Der Corregidor,* partly because of the difference in genre. The knowledge that the musical close will be followed by the boundary of silence gives a quite different perspective to a song's insistence upon the tonic. It becomes the absolute defining goal for the song instead of being an intermediate point of reference as in the opera. Within the enclosing symmetries of phrase and key in *Auch kleine Dinge*, any hesitations of rhythm and harmony acquire a magnified existence, as one listens for any possibilities of expansion beyond the four-bar phrase. In the prelude the right and left hands of the piano entertain a dialogue about where the main rhythmic stress falls, on the first and third or the second and fourth beats of the bar, an issue which is only clarified by the rising flourish into the downbeat of bar 5. At this point a balance is achieved, the right hand of the piano filling out the textural spaces and regularly marking the half-bar within the four-bar phrases. However, echoes of the first rhythmic play continue with syncopation both in the piano's left hand and the voice, the

Example 3.1   Wolf, *Auch kleine Dinge können uns entzücken*

latter in particular showing the freedom that can come from both following a precise melodic shape and pulling away from it.

The overall descent of the song's vocal line from mediant to tonic is anticipated in the first vocal phrase. Such patterns become the opportunity for highlighting expressive details which both question and reinforce the overall direction. The C♮ of bar 5, for example, helps precipitate the first melodic descent, but then in the guise of B♯ momentarily suggests a pull back to C♯ in bars 7 and 11. If this divergence is clearly small-scale, the role of A♯/B♭ in the third vocal phrase creates a larger disturbance. The A♯ in bar 13 marks the beginning of a new ascent in the bass-line and the first pronounced sense of harmonic departure from A; a further hint of tonal escape is suggested by the vocal and harmonic concurrence upon B♭ from bars 15 to 16. The second half of bar 16 reveals such details to be part of a chromatic preparation for the arrival of the dominant E^7. However, the impact of the closing return to the first vocal phrase in bar 17 is much heightened by the new sense that the song needs to recover balance after a glimpse of tonal departure.

The song's details of containment and expansion in fact work together in a process of reaction and response, the balance between them being continually redefined. From bar 17 one might expect final closure to be imminent, the voice's reach to a high F♯ in bar 19 stressing the weight of the closing descent to A. Yet when the voice reaches the melodic A in bar 21, rhythmic and harmonic definition momentarily dissolve beneath it; the voice's rhyming cadence-point is elided with a return to the prelude and its shifting textures and stresses. The familiarity of this prelude material and the anticipation of its closing on A, in its turn, compensate for the momentary shift in the listener's expectation. However the shift means that even in this final enactment of closure the song's symmetries are bound in with an impression of unexpected openness, 'small things' resonate with a larger significance than might at first appear – as the poem so aptly expresses.

This song proclaims a message which in fact is borne out, though often in highly contrasting ways, by nearly all of Wolf's songs – the message that the greatest expressive significance is to be found in tracing the precise details of musical closure. For then possibilities for expansion are measured against a carefully defined and realised musical goal. In many ways the composer thus identified himself with the essential nature of the Lied as a closed genre, turning its restriction into an opportunity for heightened expression. Walter Niemann in his book *Die Musik seit Richard Wagner* of 1913 indeed characterised Wolf as a conservative in his approach to song, even while he also identified him as the creator of the modern Lied.[5] For in Niemann's opinion Wolf succeeded in creating a balance between the traditional and the radical, the natural boundaries of the Lied and the wish for musical development and expansion, a balance that was later pulled apart. This notion of balance is an apt one; however, Niemann falls short of recognising that Wolf's formal conservatism, his concern with closure, was in fact his means of innovation. So much of the debate about Lieder in the later nineteenth century was concerned with marking out an opposition between folk-like ideals for the genre – as manifested in closed strophic or ternary forms and clearly defined melodies – and freer dramatic styles as influenced by Wagnerian music drama. It as though song criticism had still failed to move beyond the initial debates aroused by Goethe's ideas for the genre of the lyric and his uncompromising demands that song-settings follow an unchanging strophic form, simple syllabic melodies and simple chordal accompaniments, to allow the words to shine through without musical distractions. Such strictures were usually honoured in the breach, Schubert's songs establishing the status of the genre by the incursion of dramatic musical features taken from opera and cantata.[6] Yet Goethe's demands were still held up as the ideal, even when there was little actual musical practice that could demonstrate their fruitfulness. Even Schubert's relatively simple strophic song *Heidenröslein* failed to follow a purist definition of the Lied as one might see in Koch's *Musikalisches Lexicon* of 1802; Koch believed that the vocal line should have no 'extended syllables as characterize the artificial and cultivated aria' and should be 'capable of being performed by anyone who has healthy and not entirely inflexible vocal chords'.[7] Hermann Kretzschmar in his later studies of the nineteenth-century Lied continued to summarise the aim of song-composers as being to make their music 'as folk-like as possible',[8] an ideal that indeed began to seem the more precious because of the threatening influence of Wagnerian music drama. For according to Kretzschmar, the genre of music drama encouraged overflowing piano parts to swallow up the voice and dry declamation to replace living song.[9] Brahms agreed with such opinions, stating in a letter to Clara Schumann 'the Lied is now sailing so false a course that one cannot hold fast enough to the ideal – and that for me is folk-song'.[10]

For Brahms the folk ideal actually assumed an unusual degree of substance, the composer conforming to the literal forms and styles of folk-song in certain collections and thus giving himself a concrete measure for the musical practice of his more developed songs. There is a clear stylistic distinction between the two types of song-composition, but for once the 'ideal' had been grounded in practice and specific aspects carried over into the more advanced style.[11] Ironically enough Wagner and the Wagnerians also paid homage to an ideal of folk-song, but usually saw it by contrast as something untouchable, shrouded in nostalgic reference to the German past and therefore not to be integrated into everyday practice. Wagner spoke enthusiastically in 'Opera and Drama' of the natural unity of words and music already achieved in ancient folk-song, where freedom of expression happened spontaneously and therefore required none of the stylistic and aesthetic revolutions involved in turning opera into music drama.[12] Yet when Wagner came to speak of the immediate present-day practice of song-composers in his brief essay on the songs of Wilhelm Baumgartner, he implied such naturalness had now been lost and the contemporary musician needed to call upon the poet's redeeming power; he must consciously seek out the melody which came not from his musical instincts but from the 'living material of the poet's verses'.[13] The terms in which he discussed the relationship between poetry and music in song were thus indistinguishable from the discussions surrounding music drama. Critics such as Heinrich Schuster, writing in the pages of *Bayreuther Blätter*, were encouraged to describe the Lied as its own kind of *Gesamtkunstwerk*, even though only the arts of poetry and music were involved without the scenic aspects of music drama. Schuster praised the song-composer Robert Franz, known to be admired by Wagner, for creating a true 'speech-melody' and for employing leitmotifs in a way analogous to the master.[14]

The specific connections between Franz and Wagner proposed by Schuster – he even went so far as to make comparisons between particular songs of Franz and sections from Wagner's music dramas – contrast strikingly with Franz's own thoughts on his song-practice. He described his songs as combining modern piano styles with Baroque polyphony, and as seeking to balance the 'ideal' with the 'realistic'. His concern for clearly defined forms provided the realistic frame for his music, for as he said 'it is a tricky matter to decide between musical and poetic factors . . . and one cannot manage without compromises'. He criticised those who sought to apply Wagnerian declamation directly to song, saying prosodic declamation was often given too much weight by post-Wagnerian composers.[15] Indeed the preponderance of simple piano textures and rhyming vocal phrases in his songs reveals his continuing respect for the ideals of independent melody and folk-like expression.

Thus although Franz's songs were claimed by the Wagnerians as a product of music drama, in practice they show that the composer needed more definite models; he himself declared that Schubert and Bach were the main influence on his songs, not Wagner.[16] Hans Sommer is perhaps a more straightforward example of a purely Wagnerian song-writer, showing in his one-act opera on Nordic legends *Der Meermann* of 1895 that he was quite prepared to follow Wagner closely in style and spirit. The opening evocation of the sea owes much to Wagner's Rhine and the children proceed to sing dance-like songs in imitation of the Rhinemaidens. Then their play is disturbed by the appearance of the Meermann, much like that of Alberich in *Das Rheingold*. The overall dramatic content of the story also owes much to Wagner, being concerned with the Meermann's need of redemption from a curse, and – like *Die Meistersinger* – with an allegory on the nature of music. For the Meermann is cursed for saying that the power of his song is greater than the power of the gods – 'Nun giebt's in der Welt nur einen Gott: mein lachender Liederklang' (Now there is only one god in the world – the sound of my laughing song). The children turn away from the Meermann in horror, calling him a monster, but the heroine Agnete pleads with them, saying they should pity him, for he who sings so beautifully must have a soul.

Her song is seen as working the beginning of the Meermann's salvation. And indeed throughout the opera song, in the sense of a simple triad-based melody with rhyming periodic phrases, is treated as having magical powers, imbuing its hearers with wisdom and insight. The hero Ingolf comes to the Meermann to hear him sing and to be given a vision of the future. As Friedrich von Hausegger has pointed out, according to the Nordic myths he who sings is also a seer or prophet.[17]

Example 3.2   Hans Sommer, 'Der Lenz ist gekommen', *Lieder aus Julius Wolff's Minnesang Tannhäuser*, Op. 5 No. 1

The text for Sommer's opera was written by Hans von Wolzogen and was clearly influenced by Wagner's ideas from 'Opera and Drama' on the natural power of uncorrupted folk-song. Without the awareness of such ideas it is difficult to appreciate why Sommer's songs should have been praised so enthusiastically in the pages of *Bayreuther Blätter*.[18] For his different collections of settings of poems by Julius Wolff are full of folk-like songs which take the naive triadic style to unexpected extremes. One would have thought that the awkward declamation in the examples given here would call down scorn from Wagnerian critics, but clearly other criteria of value were at stake (see Example 3.2). Sommer was capable of a freer declamatory style, but this was explored in songs which seemed to belong to a completely different idiom (see Example 3.3).[19] Here in Example 3.3 is the opposite extreme to the folk-like settings, Sommer giving up all sense of periodic phrase and form to create a rhapsodic ramble. His songs seem to oscillate between two equally weak alternatives, both approaches endangering the integrity of the genre. For neither exploits opportunities for musical tension and surprise or gives the sense of a form being newly moulded out of the details of the material. The genre is treated as a passive framework for harmless experimentation, much as the *Bayreuther Blätter* recommended to would-be composers of music drama.

It is indeed within music drama itself that one finds the most immediate solution to Hans Sommer's weak splitting of song into unmediated extremes. For in *Die Meistersinger* in particular Wagner lays out a complete aesthetics of song based on various oppositions between closed and free forms and different kinds of reconciliation between the two. Thus the chorale at the opening of Act I sets out an ideal of

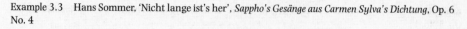

Example 3.3   Hans Sommer, 'Nicht lange ist's her', *Sappho's Gesänge aus Carmen Sylva's Dichtung*, Op. 6
No. 4

natural song-like expression, which is both self-contained and yet in its simplicity
capable of being absorbed into a broader orchestral flow. Such a balance between
musical symmetry and extension has already been demonstrated in the orchestral
prelude's contrapuntal treatment of simple hymn-like material. And even at the
beginning of Act I the orchestra appears ready to resume the flow with the links that
it offers to the chorale's phrases.

Die Meistersinger's initial notion of balance is disturbed both by Walther's insistence on entirely free-flowing song in his first test in front of the Meistersingers in Act
I scene 3 ('So rief der Lenz in den Wald') and by the contrastingly fussy rhyming
phrases of Beckmesser's serenade to Eva in Act II scene 5 ('Den Tag seh' ich
erscheinen'). Walther makes a symbolic breach of the boundaries of song by incorporating the starting-signal from Beckmesser 'Fanget an!' into his actual song itself –
though the real cause of the aesthetic confusion he creates is the way his 'song'
material is not obviously different from the surrounding flow of dialogue, despite
being set off by pauses as though it were a set-piece. His treatment of song at this point
is the opposite of Hans Sachs's, for the latter breaks into balanced song-like phrases at
many points in Act II though without separating them from the surrounding texture.
His most obvious 'song', the 'Cobbling song' in Act II scene 5 ('Als Eva aus dem
Paradies'), shows him literally singing, but unlike Beckmesser in his serenade Sachs
begins as though spontaneously, mid-flow in his tune, and has little trouble improvis-
ing and spinning out his phrases . His text is also improvised to form a commentary to
the action around him.

Hans Sachs is thus identified with the orchestral prelude's balance between closure

Example 3.4   Wagner, 'Prize song', *Die Meistersinger*, Act III scene 2

and openness, representing the artistic ease of the natural born folk-singer. Through him music drama has become identified with song, or rather song has become absorbed into music drama and no longer exists as a separate genre. And yet the action of the opera still focuses upon the presentation of a set-piece, one which will re-enact Sachs's balance as a definite moment of artistic achievement. The creation of Walther's 'Prize song' remains the most important event of the work, both in showing the hero's reach to spiritual maturity and his winning of Eva, and in crowning Sachs's vision of a truly popular German art which he can offer to the people. The pauses which surround the 'Prize song' as it first emerges in Act III scene 2 are clearly intended to help emphasise the self-contained symmetry of the phrases, in a manner analogous to the chorale at the opening of Act I. However, a closer look at the phrases themselves reveals that the sequential movement within them is directed more to encouraging melodic extension than symmetrical balance (see Example 3.4).

One is not surprised to learn that Wagner first conceived the 'Prize song' without words; the flow of phrases hardly lends itself to dwelling on individual details of declamation. Although presented as a song, the material here is actually an example of one of Wagner's fluent motivic extensions, a quasi-symphonic flow which can be fixed and suspended at any point. The pauses confirm this skilful ability of the composer to suspend and then smoothly pick up his motivic fabric but they are always sensed as an artificial boundary. Even when the intermediate pauses are removed as Walther sings the song to Eva in Act III scene 4, one wants the motivic flow to expand further. Thus when Walther presents his final version to the crowd in Act III scene 5 with an enthusiastic spilling over of new phrases, this is the already anticipated resolution of the nature of the 'Prize song'. Rather than performing a song and then showing its potential for indefinite expansion, Walther has caught a section of free-flowing fantasy, successfully held it in suspension for a moment and then let it return to its more natural state. Walther's 'Prize song' holds up the language of music drama for the praise of the crowd. He thus comes at the balance of contained and free musical expression from a different direction to Sachs, and Sachs welcomes him as the renewal of an old order. If Sachs is the representative of the natural folk-singer, then Walther rescues song from the potential perversions of Beckmesser and replaces song with music drama. The ideal of song takes centre stage in *Die Meistersinger*, but only in the end to be absorbed as a metaphor for the language of music drama.

Example 3.5   Wilhelm Baumgartner, *Noch sind die Tage der Rosen*

In the rest of Wagner's music dramas there are plenty of other examples where the composer accords song a symbolic status, invoking the notion of a clear musical and dramatic boundary within which truth is revealed or power exercised. One thinks for example of the spell cast on the hero by Kundry's narration about his mother in Act II of *Parsifal* or the truths imparted by the Woodbird's song in Act II of *Siegfried*. However, these song-sections essentially achieve their significance by the way they contrast with their musico-dramatic surroundings, creating a build-up of tension as one waits for the release from their exaggerated calm. One thinks how Parsifal violently repulses Kundry and Siegfried bursts out with even greater energy in response to the Woodbird. The crucial patterns of musical tension and resolution build up around rather than within the song-section, while in itself the section offers a kind of musico-dramatic safe haven. Tristan's song-like vision of Isolde in Act III scene 1 of *Tristan und Isolde*, 'Wie sie selig', is striking for the way in which the chromatic language of the opera achieves a magical repose in E major. The harmonic sonorities

Example 3.6   Hans Sommer, 'Du kommst zu mir in Traume', *Hunold Sinuf*, Op. 4

which have been used throughout the work now appear free from the tonal uncertainties and ambiguities usually surrounding them, instead helping decoratively to underline the stable rocking movement of a lullaby.

Such contrasts surrounding the use of song-like sections work most effectively within the wider context of Wagner's music dramas, but the passivity he assigned to song weakens the musical status of the genre when it is considered by itself. The material of Wagner's *Wesendonck Lieder*, for example, appears strikingly less significant when presented in this format than when appreciated in the context of *Tristan und Isolde*. Taken by themselves the sinking chromatic lines of 'Träume' reveal a rather predictable evocation of mood for a lyrical set-piece, colourfully encircling the tonic without disturbing the sense of stasis. Wilhelm Baumgartner introduced a similar pattern in the piano prelude to his simple strophic song *Noch sind die Tage der Rosen* (It is still the days of roses) (see Example 3.5).[20] The magical *Tristan* harmonies – so full of significance in the music drama as the first point of emotional settling after extended passages of apparently irresolvable chromatic and rhythmic disturbance – seem in the song in danger of falling into a comfortable sentimentality and of offering a too obvious definition of emotion. One notes how easily Hans Sommer captures the same mood with similar harmonies in his song 'Du kommst zu mir in Traume' (You come to me in dreams) from the collection *Hunold Sinuf* (see Example 3.6).[21]

Wolf consistently waged war on any such temptations to turn song into a vehicle for emotional sentimentality, revitalising the impact of such material by the radical nature of his harmonic exploration. Yet his attack against limited views of song was also aimed at more fundamental issues of musical treatment and approach. In the Italian songs in particular Wolf questioned the kind of effect a closed boundary might

Example 3.7   Wolf, *Wenn du mich mit den Augen streifst*

have upon the development of musical material and the kind of possibilities it left open for musical expression. Instead of limiting the potential for dramatic enactment of a text, excluding dramatic tensions to beyond the boundaries of song, Wolf made a closed formal boundary a cue for their inclusion within the immediate development of the material. The battle to find a balance between formal symmetries and formal expansion was drawn up within song, rather than around it.

In the Italian songs the battle for musical control is often pinned to one particular detail of harmony or melody since so much in the songs seemed carefully circumscribed. Indeed in *Wenn du mich mit den Augen streifst* (When you look at me with your eyes) Wolf seems at first to be adopting the settled melodies and gentle nostalgic air of other unchallenging late nineteenth-century song styles. The lilting rhythms and decorative leans towards the relative minor and back suggest a straightforwardly sentimental avowal of love (see Example 3.7 on previous pages). The rise and fall of chromatic details in the harmonic texture seem designed to emphasise the arch-like balance of the piano's melody. However, from bar 9 of the song the melody and harmony shift in relation to each other to disrupt the immediate sense of answering two-bar phrases. The containment is thus not to be taken for granted; it is a sign of the calm that the poet wishes to assume but which is actually under threat with one look from his beloved's eyes. The chromatic steps which seemed so innocuous in the first half of the song become in the second half part of a continually expanding arch which is in danger of losing its central point of balance around the tonic G. The passing resolution at the beginning of bar 13 offers some harmonic direction by outlining the dominant D, but the subsequent E♭s in bars 13 and 14 also suggest a quite different tonal goal. Within the single climactic sequence of bars 15 to 16 Wolf compresses a startling change in perspective, the A♭ triad in bar 15 seeming to clinch an escape from harmonic containment but the subsequent G asserting a bigger tonal sweep that encloses A♭ as a Neapolitan sixth within a return to the tonic. The further shift to an A^7 chord in bar 16 meets the previous flatward move with an opposing one sharpwards, the speed of these harmonic changes underlining the urgency of the need to assert tonal balance. The final measured steps to resolution on G in bar 17 and the closing echoes of the first lilting oscillations in the piano postlude confirm that imbalance has indeed been averted.

After all, as one notes from the poem, the speaker is only warning his beloved of his heart bursting apart as a conceit to underline the intensity of his love. Yet in Wolf's setting the expression of his passion has certainly transcended the sentimental and conventional level one suspected at the beginning. The first small-scale circling around G is replaced by a far more penetrating exploration of the boundaries of tonal containment. The movement to closure succeeds in unleashing a sense of the song's large-scale tonal direction, its power as a single shape rather than as a series of finely etched chromatic movements. The return to G in bar 15 opens out a new and unexpected sense of scale, even while underlining the song's closed formal boundary.

On the surface it seems highly contradictory that the poet's reference to 'breaking out' (ausbrechen) should be interpreted by Wolf as a return to the tonic triad; one can imagine what Wagner might have done with such a poetic phrase. But in fact Wolf's way of using the tonic triad climactically within the confines of song effectively conveys simultaneous messages of closure and expansion. Such a song thus gives ample evidence of the expressive tensions capable of being released and resolved within the Lied. In contrast to Wagner's symbolism of song the Italian songbook shows Wolf drawing immediate power back to the genre, illuminating the ideal of simple and enclosed musical expression by a precise realisation of its powers and limitations. His songs thus transcend the categories of style and form which had grown up around the Lied through the nineteenth century and offer in their place a radical reformulation, based upon his appreciation of the essential realities of the genre and an uncompromising view of the integrity of musical language. For against expectations of the time, song in Wolf's hands became a primary test of a composer's powers of musical coherence, a test which in its own way matched the scope of music drama and brought song into a whole new area of aesthetic debate and exploration.

Chapter four

'Poetry the man, music the woman'? Wolf's reworking in his Mörike songs of Wagner's aesthetics of words and music

When late nineteenth-century critics found themselves faced with the often unnerving challenge of Wolf's music, applying Wagner's aesthetic formula – 'poetry is the man, music the woman' – offered them an immediate way of making sense of the impact of his songs. While acknowledging that it was hard to trace the logic of Wolf's harmonies, or identify a consistent stylistic character in his music, they could agree that such difficulties were serving poetry and bringing individual poems to life.

And this, for some, was the only critical appreciation they thought Wolf needed. The stories abound from first-hand observers, such as Hermann Bahr and Friedrich Eckstein, of how the composer would immerse himself in particular poems, and then write his settings with lightning speed, as though 'inspired'. With such a view, it seemed inappropriate to critics to question how the composer's interpretations arose, it was sufficient to value the poetic end result. In one of the earliest articles on Wolf's songs, Josef Schalk's 'Neue Lieder, neues Leben' of 1890, the writer stressed the 'naturalness' of Wolf's music and how it appeared as a spontaneous bloom from the 'roots' of German folk-art.[1] Wolf's music and the poetry were 'destined' for each other, as in folk-song, as in Wagnerian music drama, and clearly any notion of artistic calculation must not be allowed to disturb such a 'love-bond'. Wagner admitted that 'musical need' determined some of his own union with poetry, the need to find a channel for his expansions of Beethoven's symphonic language. But throughout 'Opera and Drama' Wagner claimed this was paralleled by poetry's needs to find a new emotional voice, thus restoring the sense of a 'natural' balance between the arts.[2]

Of course, the 'poet' existed in Wagner's music dramas only in a hypothetical sense, since the text did not exist artistically apart from its potential for musical realisation; the 'poet' was essentially only another voice for Wagner the musician. Yet far from endangering Wagner's 'love-bond', the playing out of the roles of 'poetry the man, music the woman' within the aesthetic sphere of *music* allowed Wagner to assume the sense of inevitability that was the hallmark of the *Gesamtkunstwerk*. If the poetic text had been recognised as a separate entity, then the composer would have had to engage in complex negotiations of detail and structure, which would have raised disturbing reflections on the nature of poetic versus musical communication. And Wagner's whole aim, as expounded most clearly in 'The Music of the Future', was to answer the question 'why' that he thought was evoked by Beethoven's symphonic music, or at least to provide powerful assertions that made questions of purpose seem irrelevant.

Recognising the close relationship which Wolf created between music and poetry, early critics looked for a similarly unquestionable source for his achievements and sought to place Wolf within the bounds of poetry. 'Wolf the musician' became in his turn an almost hypothetical person, since one of the most common ways of describing the success of his songs was 'Wolf became the poet.'[3] It is conceivable that writers might have reversed the direction of this bonding and shown Wolf as musician appropriating the poetry, or recreating the poet in his own image. If one looks at the poets he chose, beginning with Mörike and Goethe, it would not be hard to reinterpret them as spokesmen for Wolf's musical needs. Wolf had known Mörike's poetry since 1878, but as he began the Mörike songbook in 1888 he clearly relished the opportunity to use some of his psychologically tormented poems as vehicles for Wagnerian chromatic harmony. This was the first time Wolf had introduced such a Wagnerian style into his songs, and the variety of subject matter and treatment in Mörike's poetry allowed him the chance to explore the style's many aspects and assimilate it in various ways within the confines of the Lied. From these Mörike songs a musical formal discipline began to emerge which Wolf then sought to refine in the Goethe songbook. And again one might see the choice of Goethe's poetry, with all its formal challenges and perfection, as determined by the course of the composer's musical development.

Wolf's purely musical initiatives became yet more obvious with the Spanish and Italian songbooks which followed, where the quality of the poetry was arguably lower. However, critics have always been reluctant to consider Wolf's musical instincts independently of poetry. This may be partly because, seen by themselves, his instincts moved in unexpected directions, away from Wagner and away from late nineteenth-century conventional ideas of musical progress. Musically speaking, Wolf's songs presented the inevitability of formal closure, enacted in precise terms irrespective of the immediate nature of the stylistic material. His musical structures pushed against many nineteenth-century notions of 'transcendence', and imposed a formal view which at times could be even workmanlike and prosaic. His formal habits were indeed surprisingly neutral; structural closure did not invariably bring associations with 'the inevitability of death' or a nostalgia for childhood as in the songs of Mahler. Wagner in his music dramas almost always imbued notions of formal openness and closure with poetic qualities of 'spiritual' versus 'earthbound' perspectives. However, in Wolf's songs, musical closure did not have an in-built poetic message; this had to be negotiated from an interaction with the particular poem, and Wolf was constantly unfolding new and surprising associations for his forms. In emphasising closure Wolf made it clear he was upholding the realities of the genre within which he was working, rather than asserting an expressive musical personality. Such neutrality – Wolf liked to call himself 'an objective lyricist'[4] – would have been chilling to a late-Romantic consciousness, and it is perhaps not surprising that critics asserted that Wolf 'became' Mörike or Goethe.

However, artistic neutrality or objectivity is different from artistic passivity. And while one might agree that Wolf was fully caught up in aiding the poet's expressive message rather than his own, one should not underestimate the composer's passionate interest in exploring how he might achieve that end. Unlike Wagner, Wolf wanted his listeners to be aware of the musical choices he was making and the negotiations that led to each end result, and he prevented them from taking any aspect of his interpretations for granted. He sought to arouse a critical faculty in his audience, as a reflection of his own passionate criticism of poetry, whereas according to Nietzsche Wagner demanded 'obedience' from his listeners, not thought:

> Above all, no thought! Nothing is more compromising than a thought. Rather the state preceding thought, the throng of yet unborn thoughts, the promise of future thoughts, the world as it was before God created it – a recrudescence of chaos. – Chaos induces intimations.[5]

From a later critical standpoint, Theodor Adorno believed that if audiences of the music dramas were to depart from their music-induced state of intoxication for a moment of critical reflection, Wagner's illusion of an 'ideal unity' in the *Gesamtkunstwerk* would be shattered.[6] Adorno saw Wagner as caught up in the 'magic' of his musico-poetic synthesis and wanting his audiences to be so too:

> The dreamer encounters his own image impotently, as if it were a miracle, and is held fast in the inexorable circle of his own labour, as if it would last for ever. The object he has forgotten he has made is dangled magically before his eyes, as if it were an absolutely objective manifestation.[7]

If it was Wolf's purpose to reawaken audiences to the actual processes of creation which underlay a musician's role as poetic interpreter, then one might wonder if he had fallen outside Wagner's musico-poetic 'love-bond' altogether. However, the man–woman relationship remains a potent symbol for Wolf's bringing together of poetry and music, provided one allows notions of passionate identification to be offset by a more realistic appraisal of the difficulties of reconciling two separate identities. One is reminded of Nietzsche's scornful correction of Wagner's idealistic view of love-relationships:

> Artists do what all the world does . . . they misunderstand love. Wagner, too, misunderstood it. They believe one becomes selfless in love because one desires the advantage of another human being, often against one's own advantage. But in return for that they want to *possess* the other person.[8]

To Nietzsche, love was often 'war – and at bottom the deadly hatred of the sexes!' Such hard-headed realism was antipathetic to the dissolving of identity that was so powerfully enacted in Wagner's *Tristan und Isolde* – both in the love between the two characters, and in terms of the work's musico-poetic relationships. For, as has often been pointed out, nothing really happens in Wagner's *Tristan* except psychological exploration through music of the given circumstances, leaving the surface of the poetry to wait upon the music and to become little more than generalised padding. In *Tristan* the 'spirit of music' was now the avowed source for both poem and music, as Wagner outlined in his essay 'Beethoven' of 1870.

Wolf, for his own part, said he found something horrible and vampire-like in the tendency of music to swallow up poetry.[9] And indeed when he performed his own songs he insisted on each poem being read out loud first. Such a performance practice was highly provocative, and it is not surprising that it happens rarely today. Goethe asked that song-composers respect the independent musicality of his verses, and leave the singer to bring out the various shifts of poetic rhythm and meaning. But this was an entirely different matter from an audience hearing the poem spoken first, and then sung in its musical interpretation. Such proximity allowed one to appreciate how cleverly Wolf aligned his vocal declamation to the fluctuating intonations of speech. But it also brought home how these fluctuations were now caught and made part of a separate coherent musical realisation. Wolf invited his audience to appreciate the accuracy and care of his critical responses, but he was also reminding them of the change of medium that was taking place and preventing them fostering the illusion that the poems emerged from his music 'as if for the first time'.

Wolf often said that a musician's work had to be kept distinct from a poet's work, and he believed – except perhaps in the case of Wagner, who was 'always something else'[10] – that it was a dangerous gift to be both poet and musician.[11] Wolf's idea of the musician's work in a song was clearly to capture a response to something artistically finished, a poem that would need 'unpicking' through music, before being reassembled as a new creation ready for comparison with the original. The tension between detail and form which Wolf appreciated in the poem had to be recreated in musical terms, if he was to do justice to the poem as it stood. 'Obedient' musical reflections in the spirit of Goethe were not sufficient. Indeed Wolf often seemed to avoid obvious connections between music and poetry that would allow listeners to hear his music as simply descriptive.

By the late nineteenth century it was the conventional wisdom that Lieder composers should concentrate upon evoking a mood in their musical setting to connect with the underlying mood of the poem.[12] This linking mood was often strengthened by the presence of a recurring musical motif, which drew upon some specific poetic image and helped the development of musical form. Much as with Wagnerian leitmotifs, such a motif came to be accepted as the mediator between poetic and musical meaning and the key to the composer's interpretation. Thus the song's initial moments of motivic encapsulation were usually seen as crucial to its conception, the rest being simply a matter of formal follow-through. Yet Wolf was quite prepared to disturb this practical and effective scheme of musico-poetic interaction for ones that were far more unpredictable in their execution. Quite often in the Mörike songbook, Wolf avoided establishing a clear sense of mood or a characteristic motif altogether until the later stages of the song, leaving one to follow his thoughts first through various dark turnings. If the song did offer a clear motif initially, this sometimes contradicted the immediate character of the poem, so that again one had to wait upon later musical twists and turns in order to understand the nature of the poetic interpretation. Some of the Mörike songs were less provocative, building motivic links of a more conventional kind. But even here Wolf tended to focus upon the working out of the motif as the final arbiter of meaning, rather than making the formal treatment simply a confirmation of initial impressions.

In a simplistic way, then, one might say that Wolf had reorientated the main links between music and poetry from immediate matters of mood and motif, to a longer-term play of form and structure. However, the most crucial issue, at both these levels of interaction, was that Wolf did not merely seek obediently to follow the poetic means, closing off the distance to be bridged between music and poetry. His songs unfolded as a series of questions about the nature of musico-poetic links, rather than as statements or assertions. And these questions had to be worked through in absolute musical terms, as issues of tonality, line and rhythm, since for Wolf this reflected the reality of the medium in which he was working. The 'answer', the settling of the poetic interpretation, had to be found within musical means, even if the questions were raised through responses to poetry.

Wagner had said that music's link to poetry offered an immediate and reassuring answer to the 'why' which had emerged from within music's development. Yet Wolf presented poetry as a challenge, prompting the musician to return to issues of harmonic and formal practice, and to find coherent structures that could match poetry's expressive power and precision, from within its separate means. *Der Genesene an die Hoffnung* (The Convalescent's Ode to Hope) stands at the head of the Mörike songbook as Wolf's admission of 'the debt he owed to the poet'.[13] However, Wolf's sense of identification with Mörike did not in itself provide him with the key to the achievements of the songbook. It was rather the starting-point for a series of intense musical explorations, where Wolf's search to do duty to the poet opened up difficult questions of musical integrity which he made clear he had to answer in his own terms.

In fact *Der Genesene* is itself one of the clearest examples of Wolf daring to separate himself from the immediate mood of the poem and embarking upon an unexpected musical narrative. Eric Sams has pointed out how the triumphalism of the song's first climax contradicts the poem's overriding mood of penitence.[14] Mörike's poem absorbs reference to the past struggle with death and the spiritual blindness which followed, as background to a present plea for forgiveness and the restoration of spiritual health:

Der Genesene an die Hoffnung

Tödlich graute mir der Morgen:
Doch schon lag mein Haupt, wie süss!
Hoffnung, dir im Schoss verborgen,
Bis der Sieg gewonnen hiess.
Opfer bracht' ich allen Göttern,
Doch vergessen warest du;
Seitwärts von den ew'gen Rettern
Sahest du dem Feste zu.

O vergib, du Vielgetreue!
Tritt aus deinem Dämmerlicht,
Dass ich dir ins ewig neue,
Mondenhelle Angesicht
Einmal schaue, recht von Herzen,
Wie ein Kind und sonder Harm;
Ach, nur einmal ohne Schmerzen
Schliesse mich in deinem Arm!

[*The Convalescent's Ode to Hope*

Day dawned deathly pale:
But my head already lay sweetly resting,
Hope, hidden in your lap,
Until the victory was won.
I brought sacrifices to all the gods,
But you were forgotten;
Aside from the eternal rescuers
You watched the ceremony.

Oh forgive, thou ever-faithful!
Come out of your shadows,
So that I can look in your ever new
Moonbright face
Once, with all my heart,
Like a child and without grief;
Oh, just once, free from pain,
Enclose me in your arm!]

Yet what was background in Mörike's poem first appears definitely as foreground in Wolf's setting. The opaque harmonies of bars 2 and 4 frustrate the sense of purpose in the song's opening rhythmic sequences, and offer a graphic depiction of the speaker's struggle against death (see Example 4.1). The glimmer of tonal definition in bar 7, with the first recognisable triadic sonority of E major, then releases a series of directional impulses which seem to convey the effect of life returning with the dawn. The voice responds to the piano's harmonic clarification with a moment of

Example 4.1   Wolf, *Der Genesene an die Hoffnung*

melodic definition, and this leads to a dialogue of harmonically and melodically connecting sequences, quickening to the climax of bar 13.

The descriptive power of this textural growth is unassailable, yet the tonal foundations of the passage remain strikingly slim. The E major of bar 7 does relate to tenuous suggestions of C♯ minor within the piano prelude; but it owes its power to a surface change of textural presentation rather than a broader tonal continuity. The ominous pause in bar 16 at the top of the piano's E major fanfares is an accurate reflection of the song's lack of underlying tonal direction at this point, as are the steps tracing a return to the song's first octave C♯s in bar 18. Here the descriptive sequences of the

Example 4.1 (*cont.*)

[melodic resolutions]   [40]

Gb major

song's first section are cast aside in favour of dwelling upon the initial movement from C♯ to F♯ in bars 1 and 2, now interpreting them more clearly as a step from dominant to tonic. The obscuring D♯ of bar 2 re-emerges in the bass-line in bar 19, delaying the tonal establishment of F♯/G♭ until the beginning of bar 22. However, the extending step-wise movement of bars 1 and 2 – C♯, D♯, E, E♯/F – is now rationalised as preparation for an intermediate cadence on B♭ minor in bar 21. The opposition between G♭ and B♭ might seem to reawaken the song's first sense of fluctuating tonality. But in fact when B♭ reappears in bar 25 in the major, it becomes clear that it has a dominant-style function within an implied E♭ minor, helping prepare for the crucial return to G♭ as tonic in bar 28. Indeed if one now measures out the tonalities of the song around a framework of major/minor equivalents, it becomes clear that even the earlier E major can be seen in retrospect as part of a series of dominant-style tonalities preparing for this moment:

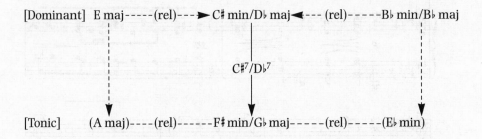

The section from bars 18 to 28, while this tonal direction is waiting to be confirmed, presents an effective analogue to the picture of the poet wandering off to false gods while Hope waits for his spiritual blindness to be dispelled. Yet the terms of this depiction are still based on a tonal logic which is pursuing its own course without specific reference to the poem. It is only as the settling on G♭ major in bar 28 coincides with 'O vergib' – the poet's first direct appeal to Hope – that one senses an immediate and inextricable bonding between music and poem. And in some senses this is where the 'song' proper begins. The motif from bars 7 and 8 now takes up its role as a constant rhythmic and melodic presence, while the still ranging harmonies are drawn into a unified course by the balanced arches of the periodic phrasing.

From dramatic enactment the song has settled into an expressive lyricism, such as one might have expected from initially surveying the poem. Typically Wolf has chosen to rouse his listeners, by showing his song seeking out a kind of expression that might otherwise have been taken for granted. Yet the consequences of the manner of his musical interpretation do not stop here. The final phrase of the song from bar 34 no longer suggests a plea for restoration, it takes a step further and introduces an exaggeratedly peaceful melodic and harmonic close, as though Hope had already responded and enfolded the soul in its arms. Taken by itself, this would seem to break once more the present mood of the poem. But musically, such a conclusion is precisely poised to balance the tonal disturbances of the song's first half and confirm the tonic G♭. The observation that the composer has moved beyond the poem is actually dwarfed by a larger appreciation of his power to complete his musical analogue with a point of absolute resolution, and thus offer the song in its entirety as a reading of the poem.

Wolf's setting of *Denk es, o Seele!* (Consider, O my Soul!) is a similarly challenging example of the composer making the listener wait until the final section of the song to settle the basis of his poetic interpretation. This might seem surprising, since this song opens with a prominent motif which encapsulates the sense of mystery at the heart of the poem. The motif works at a descriptive level, the bare B♭ octaves suggesting a tolling funeral bell and the answering melodic fragment a transient memory of life, tinged by sinking chromaticism which comes like a premonition of mortality (see Example 4.2).

Such an ambiguous pairing, in the song's first five bars, of musical images which both stand apart from each other and belong together sums up the poem's provocative juxtaposition of life and death. For Mörike links images of nature with images of the grave, even though one feels they ought to be kept separate:

Denk es, o Seele!

Ein Tännlein grünet wo, wer weiss, im Walde,
Ein Rosenstrauch, wer sagt, in welchem Garten?
Sie sind erlesen schon, denk es, o Seele,
Auf deinem Grab zu wurzeln und zu wachsen.

Zwei schwarze Rösslein weiden auf der Wiese,
Sie kehren heim zur Stadt in muntern Sprüngen.
Sie werden schrittweis gehn mit deiner Leiche;
Vielleicht, vielleicht noch eh' an ihren Hufen
Das Eisen los wird, das ich blitzen sehe!

[*Consider, O my Soul*

A little fir-tree grows in the wood, who knows where,
A rose-bush in a garden, who can say which?
They are already chosen, consider, O my soul,
To take root and grow on your grave.

Two little black horses graze in the meadow,
They come back to town at a gay trot.
They will go step by step with your coffin;
Perhaps even before they lose the iron from their shoes,
That now I see flashing before me.]

In summing up the juxtaposition of life and death in his song's piano prelude, Wolf might be said to have reduced the shock value of the poem's change in tone from folk-like nature imagery halfway through the first stanza. However, the poem makes clear

Example 4.2   Wolf, *Denk' es, o Seele!*

Example 4.2 (cont.)

Example 4.3   Wolf, *Denk' es, o Seele!* (bars 1–10)

it is dealing with certainties – the roses have already been chosen for the grave, these horses will carry the coffin. It is thus quite appropriate poetically that the musical mood of the prelude's motif should encompass the whole song. And apart from the motivic return mid-way in bar 27 and at the close in bar 55, the two halves of each verse can be easily related to the two halves of the prelude's motif, though in reverse order. The vocal phrases of bars 11 and 12, and bars 33 to 36, follow the profile of the second half of the prelude motif, while the tolling bass octaves from halfway through each verse, bars 19 and 43, relate to the song's first two bars.

Superficially, then, Wolf is following a conventional nineteenth-century model in *Denk es, o Seele!*, allowing the song to develop out of the extension of a single mood and a single motif. The musical fractures that appear with the sudden contrasts of texture, tonality and rhythmic style at the halfway point in each verse can be understood as the reflections of the fractures within the motif, and thus not endangering the song's formal unity or its links with the poem. Even the moment of tonal and registral disjuncture, from the end of the prelude to the beginning of the verse in bar 11, helps the motif perform its characteristic function. If the verse began smoothly in F major, then the prelude's sequence ending on C^7 in bar 10 would seem to have moved away from the first suggestion of D minor, whereas in fact the return to D minor in bar 11 negates any sense of formal direction. The prelude is seen to revolve in a circle harmonically, the chromatic movements outlined from bars 4 to 5 and then from bars 9 to 10, in fact bringing the sequence of intervallic pitches back to where it started (see Example 4.3).

This circular harmonic motion helps bind the prelude's contrasts together, and promises to do the same for the song as a whole. The quick inflexions from D minor to D major in bars 11 and 12 of the verse, and then the switch to F major in bars 13 to 15, continue to suggest an easy fluctuation between major and minor. Although the omnipresence of the motif's harmonic patterns brings constant reminders of death, it also offers a certain reassurance. As long as thoughts of death are conveyed through defined images, they can be entertained quite comfortably in the present, just as the poet dwells with loving care on his images of the fir-tree, the rose-bush and then the horses. If the poet had not included his phrase, 'Consider, O my soul', one might even imagine that the darkness of death were invoked picturesquely to heighten the brightness of such pictures from nature. And Wolf tempts his listeners to draw on this impression with the apparent ease of his harmonic fluctuations.

The song's first big contrast of bar 19 has already been texturally prepared by the prelude, and the cadence on B♭ in bar 23 also leads back harmonically to the octaves of the first bars. But the fact that this cadence is in B♭ minor rather than major for the first time inserts a crucial distance from the earlier tonalities of D minor and F major, a distance that is emphasised by the momentary suggestion of A♭ minor in bar 20. It needs all the ingenuity of semitonal voice-leading, as first introduced in the prelude's figure of bars 4 and 5, to hold such a passage together. One is no longer confident of any particular tonal orientation, until the sustained G♯ of bar 26 suggests the dominant of C♯ minor. This becomes the trigger for a return of the prelude motif in bar 27, pulling the song back on course. The motif might have been in danger of appearing rather weak and decorative here after the previous chromatic exploration; however, a tonal strand now emerges from that earlier passage to create a more substantial context for it, and for what follows. Once the harmonic and melodic pitch A re-emerges to frame bars 27 to 32, the passing tonal levels of B♭ and A♭/G♯ in the section from bar 19 become understood in retrospect as semitonal preparations for a re-establishment of the dominant. The replacement of G♯ octaves in bars 29 and 30 by A octaves in bar 32 no longer seems part of a circular and reversible harmonic motion. Instead it is a piece of directional voice-leading, showing the G♯–A–B♭–A bass-line sequence of bars 3 and 4 being transferred onto a larger tonal scale.

The larger tonal direction now associated with the song's motif is confirmed by the D minor cadence which connects the piano motif to the verse in bars 32 to 33. And Wolf continues to heighten our expectation of some definite outcome to the chromaticism of the subsequent passages, creating a greater rhythmic momentum towards the point of change in bar 43. In terms of the composer's poetic interpretation, nature images in the present have begun to seem less real to the speaker than the death which lies around the corner. The switch to a duple metre and declamatory vocal style that occurs in bar 43 might seem to depict death rising up to engulf the present and dissolve the previous clarity of vision. With a powerfully enacted funeral march, Wolf almost mocks the carefully prepared contrasts and motivic imagery of the earlier part of the song. However, musically the change is understood to have been summoned from within the material, as the initial G♯–A–B♭–A axis began to exert its directional hold. The German sixth sonority of the declamatory climax in bars 51 and 52 is clearly heard as an answer to the song's opening bars, the G♯ and B♭ pitches now clinched as part of one vertical entity preparing the close in D minor. The returning B♭ octaves in bars 55 and 57 no longer convey ambiguity, being rhythmically and harmonically tied to a new function of closure.

Looking at the beginning and end of *Denk es, o Seele!* one would say that Wolf had succeeded in retaining the motivic identity of his material, remaining true to the unity of image which gives edge to Mörike's poem. However, experiencing the song as a whole, one's view of the motivic material undergoes such a reversal that far from ensuring a lyrical containment, Wolf seems to use the motivic presence to provoke unexpected questions about the nature of his harmonic language. He is not content to leave the chromatic ambiguity of the opening to function merely in a descriptive or referential fashion. Instead the consequences of the semitonal movement are worked through at a structural level, creating contrasts in perspective that defy any easy poetic interpretation. For in the closing stages Wolf seems to transport his song into Mörike's unspoken future, while also clinging to the images which hold it to the present.

Wolf's setting of the Mörike poem *An den Schlaf* presents itself more obviously still as an investigation of the workings of Wagnerian chromatic language. The initial motif of *Denk es, o Seele!* bears comparison with the opening of Wagner's *Tristan* Prelude, in its concentration upon a French sixth-style sonority, resolving via an unexpected chromatic shift – the E♭ of bar 4 – to a dominant seventh, only to be replaced by a sequence a minor third higher. However the song's rhythmic style, its clear metrical definition and periodic phrasing, introduces a folk-like spirit quite foreign to Wagner's Prelude. *An den Schlaf*, by comparison, introduces a motif whose rocking impetus seems to grow entirely out of harmonic movements, resolving in its final bars with a clear reference to the close of Wagner's 'Liebestod' (see Example 4.4).

The resolution to E major at the end of *An den Schlaf* is prefigured by the motivic oscillation to the flat sixth F♭ in the song's opening two bars, so that the overall progression from A♭ to E could be understood as a larger reflection of the song's motivic surface. Wagner's treatment of the 'Tristan chord' in *Tristan und Isolde* is the clearest example of a single harmonic moment being projected as a long-term structural goal, the composer answering any questions of large-scale tonal continuity by drawing them back to this single reference-point. Thus the return of the 'Tristan chord' as the climax of the Prelude to Act I bears more structural weight than the re-emergence of an implied dominant preparation of A which follows in its wake, and which is soon replaced by dominant preparation of C. Similarly, the grammatical reorientation of the 'Tristan chord' in the Prelude to Act III of *Tristan* probably adds more to the music drama's processes of closure than the particular orientation to B major at the end of the 'Liebestod'. In its original statement the sonority of the 'Tristan chord' did not belong immediately within the suggested key of A minor (see Example 4.5). The sonority is recognisable within the context of more traditional functional harmony as II^7 in a minor key. If the 'Tristan chord' were respelled thus it would suggest the key of E♭ minor; indeed Wagner spells it in that fashion at the climax of the Prelude (see Example 4.6). In order to understand the progression grammatically within A minor, the melodic G♯ has to be considered as a long appoggiatura to the A at the end of the bar, thus outlining a French sixth preparing the dominant E^7. The tension of this uncertain style of resolution is removed at the beginning of the Act III Prelude, where the motivic sonority is spelled and resolved as a II^7 in F minor, inverted to II^6_5 (see Example 4.7). And this prepares for the 'Tristan chord's' clinching role in the final cadence of the 'Liebestod' (see Example 4.8).

The circling movements in Wagner's *Tristan*, the structural absorption into a

Example 4.4   Wolf, *An den Schlaf*

single harmonic reference-point, are of course a most potent realisation of the identification between life and death willed by the characters. As Tristan fervently confesses in Act III, his whole life leads him back to the mystery of what he was before birth, the 'dark' that he now wishes Isolde to draw him into forever. Such a sense of mystery hangs over Mörike's *An den Schlaf* in almost equal measure. The willing suspension of the barrier between life and death that Wagner seeks through love, Mörike finds in sleep – bringing both a lulling of the senses and the closing of the conscious mind:

Example 4.5   Wagner, Prelude to Act I of *Tristan und Isolde* (bars 1–3)

Example 4.6   Wagner, Prelude to Act I of *Tristan und Isolde* (bars 82–5)

Example 4.7   Wagner, Prelude to Act III of *Tristan und Isolde* (bars 1–4)

Example 4.8   Wagner, final bars of the 'Liebestod', *Tristan und Isolde*

An den Schlaf

Schlaf! süsser Schlaf! obwohl dem Tod, wie du, nichts gleicht,
Auf diesem Lager doch willkommen heiss' ich dich!
Denn ohne Leben so, wie lieblich lebt es sich!
So weit vom Sterben, ach, wie stirbt es sich so leicht!

[*To Sleep*

Sleep! sweet sleep! Although nothing is more like death than you,
I make you welcome to this couch!
For thus without life, how lovely it is to live!
So far from dying, ah, how easy it is to die!]

Yet to Tristan and Isolde 'love' expands to make sense of all existence with no view of life or eternity outside it, whereas 'sleep' is presented as a special moment by Mörike, a unique state which allows distinctions to disappear. There is no suggestion that life and death do not retain their expected associations outside sleep or that death is not still to be feared; it is only in the likeness of sleep that death is welcomed. Mörike tightens the tension around his poetic image by requiring sleep to reconcile the irreconcilable; and sleep does so by bringing the appearance of death into life, not by exchanging the reality of one for the other.

Such differentiation between reality and appearance might seem too refined for direct musical realisation. Wolf's motivic oscillation between major and minor first presents a simpler expressive summary of the poem's ambiguity, and much of the early part of the song concentrates on bringing out how minor sonorities can be easily substituted for major. Within the chromatic inflections which follow the first melodic leans to F♭, the keys of A♭ major and minor are set alongside an equivalent pairing of C♭/B major and minor. The return of the motif in B minor at bar 9 marks the furthest point from A♭ major in the patterns of major–minor equivalence, a distinct shift to the minor as befits the poetic emphasis on death in the text at that point. This is somewhat redressed by the B major inflection in bar 11, and then by a parallel return to the motif in D♭ in bar 13, proposing an extension from A♭ that stresses the major:

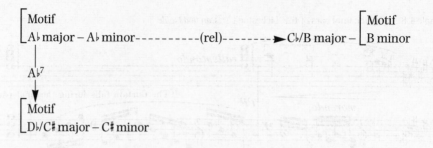

Both of these tonal moves, to B minor and D♭ major, emerge as ones that can be easily reversed to the initial A♭. And indeed once the circle is completed by the missing link, the tonal level of F♭/E (see below), one might expect that the cycle of keys could revolve indefinitely. However, Wolf's presentation of key in this song changes from the mid-point in bar 18, where the stepwise oscillations of the motif, still all-pervasive, cease to begin from points of harmonic rest. The first chords of bars 18 and 19 are dominants rather than tonics, striving towards a melodic and harmonic resolution on E which is delayed until the end of the four-bar phrase in bar 21. The D♯–E in the mid-voice of bar 18 reinterprets the E♭–F♭ of bar 1 as a directional step, instead of a decorative or fluctuating movement. Texturally, the E major of bar 21 is presented as a distinctive moment of arrival. And though the further harmonic steps to F♯ minor in bar 24 and towards A minor in bar 28 could be seen to continue the song's earlier pattern of subdominant-style shifts, these are presented by the broader periodic phrasing as moves that help define the overall orientation to E:

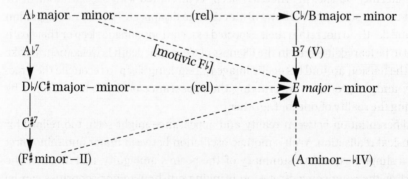

The melodic voice-leading in the final section from bar 24 suggests how the rising and falling lines of the song's motif reach towards a point of supreme balance, death and life held in mutual suspension through sleep. Yet the harmonic messages of the postlude are more specific still. The prominent melodic rise from D♯ to E of bars 28 and 29, and the harmonically incorporated shift from B to C♮ (5 to 6♭ in E) from bars 27 to 28, reawaken the inflections of the original motif. Yet such movements no longer affect the harmonic progress, here the fixing on A minor as a preparation for the cadence on E in bar 32. The 'Tristan chord' in bar 31 serves to confirm the enclosure of both the triads of F♯ minor and A minor within E major, such minor sonorities serving the major in a clear tonal hierarchy, rather than insinuating the possibility of further major/minor fluctuations.

Thus in Wolf's setting of *An den Schlaf*, the power of sleep to hold a balance between life and death is shown to come from within life, as realised through the song's emerging orientation to E major. And such a conclusion is quite distinct from Wagner's *Tristan*, despite the song's reference to the 'Liebestod'. Wolf has succeeded in honouring the specific images of Mörike's poem, while also unfolding a formal process which offers a clear tonal perspective and a precise measure for the ambiguities of Wagnerian chromatic harmony.

Taking the Mörike volume as a whole, the impression that comes out of Wolf's settings is that nothing is what it first seems. His stylistic contradiction of any simple transference of Wagner's harmonic language reflected aesthetic habits that prevented him from following the expected paths in his response to poetry. Wolf's art prospered from the power of contradiction, as much as from the expressive resources which came from his direct identification with poetry. This may seem a strange statement given the range of expressive musical imagery that one finds in the Mörike songs. However, Wolf continued to follow patterns of reversal throughout the songbook, sometimes in subtle demands on the listener, sometimes in more provocative challenges. For example, Wolf obviously enjoyed working on his two settings *Der Knabe und das Immlein* and *Ein Stündlein wohl vor Tag* side by side, on the same day,[15] and disturbing his listeners by showing how even exactly the same motivic material could be twisted to different poetic and musical outcomes.

In Wolf's setting of *Der Knabe und das Immlein* (The Boy and the Bee) the *Tristan*-style augmented-sixth sonority is repeated as part of an obsessive movement towards a cadence in G minor. And although such a motif opens the door for a sideways step to F minor in bar 5, its main role is coloristic, emphasising the minor mode (see Example 4.9). Once G minor is replaced by G major in bar 20, the sonority is allowed to be forgotten and its motivic role dissolves. Wolf interprets the description of the boy's surroundings at the beginning of the poem – the hot day, the empty broken-down house – as underlining his distance from the beloved and the yearning in his heart. But as his eyes begin to focus on the bee, he finds a messenger for his thoughts and the effect of the distance is removed. The C♯s of the French sixth turn into a trill in bar 16 just before the resolution into G major, emphasising both the turning of the boy's thoughts towards the bee and the easy assimilation of the dissonance as part of a cadential function.

Ein Stündlein wohl vor Tag (Just before Dawn) was composed immediately after *Der Knabe und das Immlein*, using exactly the same motivic sonority, again in the context of G minor. Poetically the tone is quite different, for though a swallow comes to the window with a message for the dejected speaker, she says she can hardly hear it and sends the bird away in disgust. The ease of dialogue, the game of pretend question-and-answer, in *Der Knabe und das Immlein* is here replaced by a greater concentration

Example 4.9   Wolf, *Der Knabe und das Immlein* (bars 1–27)

on the speaker's own state of mind. And it is clearly her inner torment that makes the swallow seem like a messenger rather than any actual engagement with nature or with news from the beloved:

Ein Stündlein wohl vor Tag

Derweil ich schlafend lag,
Ein Stündlein wohl vor Tag,
Sang vor dem Fenster auf dem Baum
Ein Schwälblein mir, ich hört' es kaum,
Ein Stündlein wohl vor Tag

'Hör' an, was ich dir sag',
Dein Schätzlein ich verklag':
Derweil ich dieses singen tu',
Herzt er ein Lieb in guter Ruh',
Ein Stündlein wohl vor Tag.'

O weh! nicht weiter sag'!
O still! nichts hören mag!
Flieg' ab, flieg' ab von meinem Baum!
Ach, Lieb und Treu ist wie ein Traum,
Ein Stündlein wohl vor Tag.

[*Just before dawn*

While I lay sleeping,
Just before dawn,
In the tree before my window
A swallow sang to me,
I hardly heard it,
Just before dawn.

'Listen to what I tell you,
I accuse your beloved:
While I sing this to you,
He holds another in his arms,
Just before dawn.'

Oh sorrow! Say no more!
Be quiet! I will hear no further!
Fly away! Fly away from my tree!
Ah, love and truth are just a dream,
Just before dawn.]

Wolf traces the poem's collapse inwards by disturbing the previous balance between the augmented-sixth sonority and its resolution to the dominant, D^7. In the piano prelude the augmented sixth is held for three bars and the step to the dominant is inserted only at the last moment before the introduction of the voice at the end of bar 4 (see Example 4.10).

Once the voice enters in *Ein Stündlein* it starts to follow exactly the same path as *Der Knabe und das Immlein*, though the side-step to F minor now leads to a larger-scale shift to A♭ minor, the tonality reached by reinterpreting the C♯ and E♭ of the first augmented-sixth chord as an enharmonic preparation for another dominant, E♭⁷, as appears in bars 11 and 15. The second verse is a repeat of the first, transposed to the new level of A♭ minor, though this now brings its own semitonal reorientation towards A minor, ready for the song's third verse. Concentrating on the motivic sonority by itself thus leads to a collapse of clear tonal polarities; as the poet says, all colours, all meanings, all hopes dissolve in the hour before dawn. A♭ minor or A minor are not set up in opposition to G minor. It becomes clear that any tonal modulation revolves back upon itself, without defining boundaries, when drawn from such a single ambiguous sonority. Treated in this way the augmented-sixth chord induces a kind of stasis. Such an impression is confirmed by the quick step back to G minor halfway through the third verse; the D♯ of the motivic sonority in A minor is reinterpreted as E♭ within G minor in a surprisingly seamless fashion. And the song closes by slipping back to the dominant D, the point from which it began its course at the end of the prelude.

Thus the motivic sonority of *Ein Stündlein* is finally shown to be drawn back to a semitonal relationship to the dominant D, as in *Der Knabe und das Immlein*, even though the impact of that relationship is now quite different. In the first song, the ease of the resolution to the dominant allows the motif to be left behind and forgotten. In *Ein Stündlein* there is a far stronger sense of enclosure, despite the final rhetorical imperfect cadence, because of the process of searching for other tonal outcomes which fail to materialise. The earlier song's impression of 'release' contrasts with one of 'imprisonment', as befits the change in poetic tone from the carefree passions of boyhood to the doubts and torments of maturity, from the first song's calm narrative voice to the intensity of the first person in *Ein Stündlein*.

Taking account of such poetic differences, it becomes increasingly surprising that Wolf should have used the same motivic material for both poems. There is only one other example of explicit motivic sharing in the songbook, the two *Peregrina* songs, and there the composer was reflecting the poet's own linked conception and the poems' common source in Mörike's novel *Maler Nolten*. In this other case it seems Wolf was offsetting the intense confessional tone of *Ein Stündlein* with an unexpected comparison, creating the notion of an external narrator or commentator where Mörike relied simply on the tautness of his iambic rhythms and the constant rhyming patterns of the poetic refrain to create a sense of formal stylisation. Without the comparative setting of *Der Knabe und das Immlein* one might imagine that Wolf had stayed close to Mörike, expressing the speaker's torment directly through an evocation of Wagnerian chromatic harmony and then creating a network of rhyming patterns equivalent to the poem's. Yet with his sharing of motivic material, Wolf seems

Example 4.10   Wolf, *Ein Stündlein wohl vor Tag*

to stand back from an immediate identification with the poetic content and offers a generalised response to the yearning of both lovers. The individuality of Wolf's settings of *Der Knabe* and *Ein Stündlein* has to emerge from the precise manner of their approach to formal closure, demanding a control and subtlety from the composer that surpasses the challenge of the poems themselves. In the Mörike songbook, therefore, Wolf had already moved beyond his immediate task as interpreter of neglected poems, or even as successful reinterpreter of Wagnerian harmony, and had begun to carve out an additional role for himself – one of exploring the nature of closure as a test of music's intrinsic powers of expression, or even the integrity of musical language itself.

Chapter five

The integrity of musical language – questions of form and meaning in Wolf's Goethe songs

✦

If one accepts that Wolf found a distinctive voice in his Mörike songs, then one might wonder what further challenges could lie before him in the songbooks that followed. A change of poet – from Mörike to Goethe – would only help prove the effectiveness of his interpretive powers. Some critics, such as Arthur Seidl, noted that Wolf was developing a pronounced taste for early nineteenth-century poetry and neglecting his duty as a modernist to encourage more recent poets.[1] Mörike's poems were little known in the later nineteenth century, so Wolf could claim to be bringing new works to light in his Mörike settings. But Goethe was the most familiar of writers, the father of German Romantic poetry, so that to Seidl Wolf was confirming his conservative colours by allying himself to him. Of course, as we have just seen, Wolf's artistic identity should not be seen as exchangeable with that of the poets he set; the composer could maintain a critical distance from Goethe, just as he did from Mörike. However, Wolf's choice of Goethe did have an impact on how the public saw his role as a song-writer and, as with his later choice of poetry in the Italian songbook, there does seem a sense in which he was concerned to declare more clearly what he was, by his choice of poet.

Mörike and Wolf might appear to have 'needed' each other, and the songs to have been born from a 'love-bond'; but it would be very hard to interpret the composer's interest in Goethe in that light. Goethe's own views of musical setting, his belief in the self-sufficiency of his poetry and its aesthetic distinctiveness from music, were too well known. In Goethe's opinion music belonged to a 'daemonic' sphere, apart from the immediate experience of life and immune to reason and understanding.[2] Poetry also called upon the 'daemonic' or the 'unconscious' in its effect on the emotions, but it was the business of the poet to exert his 'mental force' and to 'arrange and round off a great whole'.[3] For it was through such an 'entirety' that he spoke to the world, an entirety that was not found in Nature but created from the poet's own activity. Goethe believed the poet should absorb himself in Nature, both internal and external, but then through habits of self-concentration learn how to control it so that he was both Nature's servant and its master.[4]

It is perhaps not surprising that Goethe did not relish musicians' interference in this fine balancing of content and form, subject and object. He seems to have doubted whether composers could exert a similarly conscious control upon their material, or create an equivalent balance between form and expressive content. Formal freedom was one of Goethe's watchwords in his early fight for a German cultural identity: 'we refused to accept anything but truth and sincerity of feeling, and the quick, straightforward expression of these. Friendship, love and brotherhood, are they not voiced spontaneously?'[5] However, he treated musical freedoms suspiciously, as being without the measure of reason. If a composer set his poetry Goethe requested he keep to strophic forms; such were the rules he tried to impose.

Beethoven, for one, appreciated the significance of Goethe's distinctions between music and poetry and sought to convince the poet of both the intrinsic power of musical logic and its meaning as 'exalted symbols of the moral sense'.[6] He also consciously transgressed Goethe's strictures on song and sought to reveal interpretations that rose 'above' Goethe's poetry in his own settings.[7] As the genre of the Lied developed, such 'transgressions' almost became the norm. Yet Goethe's challenge to music's powers of internal reflection remained largely unanswered in song. Beethoven's idea for music's effect upon poetry – that melody was the 'sensual life of poetry . . . that transforms the intellectual content of a poem into pure sensation'[8] – remained the dominant aesthetic model for the development of both the Lied and Wagnerian music drama.[9] There was little suggestion that a composer might enhance the poet's formal control in a way that could add to the intellectual impact of a poem, as much as to its emotional effect. Wolf was perhaps the first song-composer to take up Goethe's implicit challenge to music, and answer it explicitly: for him the simpler question of how he might do justice to a poem became replaced by one of how he might present a balance of musical form and content that would match Goethe's own balance and articulation.

Thus, as will be seen, Wolf offered an analysis of Goethe's poetic workings as well as a realisation of the poetic end-effect, creating an air of abstraction that was often disconcertingly apparent on the surface of the Goethe songs. Many have noticed that there was a marked reduction in the range and intensity of this songbook's expressive imagery compared with the Mörike volume.[10] Goethe himself was famous for his ability to unite passion with critical detachment (he admitted to a sense of guilt as a young man for fostering love affairs to feed his artistic development). His lyrical gifts, which made Schiller cast him as a 'naive' poet of Nature, were stirred by an active consciousness that caused him to reinvoke his impressions as if he were an actor or story-teller, watching himself so as to relive and communicate his impressions with greater certainty. Often such artistic calculations were covered over by the intensity of the emotion conveyed, as in the two famous *Wandrers Nachtlied* poems. But at other times, particularly later in his life, Goethe seemed to enjoy pointing up the formal manipulation which he believed was at the heart of all poetic expression. Thus in the *Buch Suleika* of the *Westöstlicher Divan* the love affair between Hatem and Suleika is portrayed through a game that both hides and reveals the association of the cycle with Goethe's love for Marianne von Willemer, the author of the poems in Suleika's name. The two poets seek to outwit each other in their matching of poetic metre and rhyme, their spiritual union being conveyed through the combination of forms rather than just in the intensity of the language itself.[11]

In the *Schenkenbuch* from the *Westöstlicher Divan* Goethe used wine as a symbol of divine creativity, and thus characterised inspiration as an exaltation which could be summoned up by the will of the poet and experienced in the flesh as much as in the spirit. The shocking replacement of wine for the Koran as the door to eternity in *Ob der Koran von Ewigkeit sei* related to Goethe's belief in the immediacy of spiritual experience, a philosophical viewpoint which he pursued in his arguments with Schiller over whether metaphysical 'ideas' could be observed in Nature – or only seen with the spiritual eye, as Schiller believed.[12] Humour might seem inappropriate in such a philosophical context, but in fact it was one of Goethe's most important weapons. For although the humorous effect arose from his manipulation of form and language, the end result opened up questions of content and meaning that might not be expressed in any other way. Indeed Goethe's symbolic treatment of drink often evoked an impression of mystery, because for all the poet's formal virtuosity the image remained incongruous and seemed to mask a greater truth. In Goethe's eyes, perfection of form and language reflected limits of knowledge beyond which all must remain mysterious. Even in the extraordinary Harper lyrics from Goethe's novel *Wilhelm Meisters Lehrjahre*, there was no suggestion that the Harper might capture more than an echo of the final purposes of his life. The Harper focuses on his experience on this earth and his isolation from other people, patterns of experience which are traced with such certainty that they come to assume for him a fateful inevitability. He addresses 'Fate', or the 'heavenly powers', in *Wer nie sein Brot mit Tränen ass*, but the Harper's view of them is enclosed entirely by his experience, and one is left to wonder whether his life is truly under judgement from God or whether it only seems so to his diseased imagination.

In setting these Harper lyrics most composers have focused upon the awesome mystery which surrounds them, rather than the patterns which define both the form and content of the poems. Thus Schubert in his Op. 12 No. 2 version of *Wer nie sein Brot* explored an unusually wide range of enharmonically linked tonalities – from A minor/major, to F, to D♭ major – requiring large-scale repetitions of text which more than doubled the original dimensions of the poem. The strophic outline of the song was conceived by Schubert as a loose frame for his melodic and harmonic explorations, rather than as the actual basis of the expression. Such an approach would perhaps have been seen by Goethe as straying onto his territory. But in stressing the poetry's immediate lyrical aspects composers were in danger of missing the impact of the poet's dialectic with form, and therefore undercutting some of the edge and power of his creations. Wolf was not afraid to criticise the songs of his predecessors or to seek to redress what he saw as inadequacies in their treatment. He also ventured to approach poems, particularly those in Goethe's humorous or philosophical vein, that had largely been ignored by earlier composers. Therefore one might see Wolf as helping to complete an unfinished stage in the development of the Lied, rounding out the musical relationship with Goethe that was so significant to the history of the genre.

However, in the Goethe songs Wolf was also seeking to transport the Lied onto new ground, using comparison with the old to point up what was distinctive and unprecedented in his own approach.[13] In taking up the challenge of Goethe's links between content and form, Wolf betrayed a new formal consciousness – one no doubt affected by the charges of 'formlessness' laid against many late nineteenth-century composers, and against himself in his role of leading song into a post-Wagnerian future. Beethoven had answered Goethe's doubts about music by drawing the poet's attention to his symphonies,[14] but to Wolf the 'symphonic' no longer seemed such an effective measure of musical logic. Despite sympathising with the scale of intention in Bruckner's symphonies, he shared the common worry about Bruckner's powers of execution and found few coherent alternatives there to what he saw as the aridly constrained forms of Brahms's symphonic works. As a young man he had expressed great enthusiasm for Liszt's symphonic poems, but Strauss's further development of the genre in *Don Juan* evoked great scorn:

> Oh the dreary sterility of invention and affected harmonic convulsions beggar all description. Yet such music passes here as brilliant and daring. For myself I would rather be a talentless coward than such a heaven-stormer![15]

Wolf even had doubts about other composers following Wagner in his manner of appropriating symphonic tendencies. When Wolf was considering whether to follow Wagner's through-composed forms in his own operatic writing, he said he was afraid they might prove boring:

> Wagner understood this art to a tee, that is not the art of being boring, but of through-composing; however, Wagner is after all always Wagner. Us poor people cook with water and we can't allow ourselves such luxuries.[16]

Given such views it is perhaps not surprising that Wolf confined himself so much to the Lied, where the test of coherence need not be so acute. Nietzsche's dictum in the *Case of Wagner* – that musical integrity is possible only in what is small – was indeed dangerously like a counsel of despair. Nietzsche thought Wagner was himself a miniaturist who only aped the larger Beethovenian forms, and he advised musicians to turn away from pretence and withdraw entirely from symphonic dimensions. Wolf certainly followed such advice, for although critics honoured him for introducing a symphonic style of development and quasi-orchestral textures into his songs, these effects were only perceived as such because they were set within carefully contained forms. Wolf's setting of Mörike's *Der Feuerreiter* is one of the composer's most frightening evocations of raw musical power, texturally and harmonically. Yet it still draws on the immediate directional effect of the strophic refrain – 'Hinter'm Berg, hinter'm Berg, brennt es in die Mühle.' It is also noticeable that the textures lose some of their power to astonish when transferred to the orchestra in Wolf's choral version of the song.

Overall there can be little suggestion that Wolf saw it as his role to embrace symphonic logic in his songs; he was too much of a realist. But while he withdrew from that test of musical coherence, he explored others all the more. In particular, Wolf used the given boundaries of song as a chance to explore the nature of late Romantic harmonic styles, testing the links between harmonic inflexion and tonal direction as a significant basis for form. Superficially it might be possible to see Wolf as a composer who used song's closed forms as an excuse to unleash an unlimited array of harmonic colours for their immediate expressive effect, knowing that some kind of overall coherence was guaranteed. Yet Wolf believed that every one of his harsh dissonances could be justified by 'the strict rules of harmony'.[17] He was also furious when a critic said that indulgence in textural colour made some of his songs' piano parts unplayable; he vehemently denied perpetrating instrumental lunacies 'like that madman Strauss'.[18] Formal coherence for Wolf was clearly not simply a relative matter, dependent upon a particular poem or particular musical material; rather he saw it as bringing an abstract weight that could be called upon to aid the sense of meaning in a song.

One senses such a concern for formal abstraction in the ruthlessness with which Wolf treated some of the expansive stylistic textures in the Goethe songs, reducing their rich modulatory fabric to single moments of harmonic decision, in a way that might almost be in danger of seeming arbitrary or incongruous. Yet Wolf's overriding grasp of tonality and its presentation was never truly in doubt. Like Goethe, he continued to keep control over his virtuosic array of images, and was able to show the logic of stripping each song back to single points of clarification. When Goethe exerted his power in such a way it rebounded ironically on the characters or speakers in his poems, so that one had the sense of different layers of meaning – the immediate meaning coming from the speaker or characters themselves and the more subtle one from the poet/observer. The voice of the poet/observer ended up being uppermost, as though revealing a greater 'truth' behind the appearance of the material. Yet Goethe was also concerned to show how the two meanings might interact or even come together, as in the lyrics where 'speaker' and 'observer' were understood to be one. And for all the distance Goethe assumed in his ballads, by invoking a character such as Prometheus, Hatem or the Harper, the distance was only a tool of the one poet/observer and a playing out of the poetic tension of reconciling subject and object.

Wolf assumed the full burden of revealing the one meaning behind Goethe's playful multiplicity, searching for a tautness of form perhaps more appropriate to the lyric, even in the poet's most extended ballads. Commentators have praised the vividness of the composer's depiction of scene and action in his ballad settings, calling

Example 5.1   Wolf, *Gutmann und Gutweib* (bars 1–12)

them operas or plays in miniature. But this is to miss the tension that came from Wolf actually approaching such songs as lyrics, focusing from the start on a single state-ment – a statement that purported to encompass the whole but, as always with Wolf, that had to be tested and recreated through the course of the song. If one concen-trates on Wolf's description of the action itself then some of his ballads may seem dis-appointingly empty. Eric Sams praises the setting of Goethe's *Gutmann und Gutweib*, for example, for its 'verve and brilliance', its stage scenery and effects, but he says it lacks 'that deep evocation of mood or character that is the life of the Lied'.[19] Yet the true 'content' of the song is to be found in the harmonic questions raised by the ante-cedent–consequent formation of the first four bars (see Example 5.1). Bars 3 and 4 of the song seek harmonically to belie their basic function of answering the forthright statement of bars 1 and 2. Although bar 4 ends on D, the tonic outlined in the first two bars, the preceding E♭ inflexions make this seem more like a dominant than a tonic. The subdominant emphasis of bar 2 might thus be reinterpreted as part of a general tendency. The melodic patterns of falling fifths and rising fourths are picked up at a harmonic level as a lean to the subdominant, but it remains unclear whether this will encourage tonal containment or openness. In one sense the implied pattern of descending fifths in bars 1 and 2, A–D–G, offers a rational contrast to the mediant shifts of G–B–E♭ outlined from bars 2 to 4, shifts which bring semitonal juxtapositions between D and D♯/E♭, and between B and B♭. And in fact when the pattern of descending fifths is extended in the sequences from bar 5, from G to C–F–B♭–E♭, Wolf shows a way of incorporating the semitonal movements to E♭ and B♭ within a harmonic space which is clearly measured in relation to the tonic D. B♭ is indeed identified as a flat submediant substitute for D and E♭ for G in the interrupted cadence figures from bars 7 to 8, and from bars 8 to 9. For all the contrapuntal expansiveness of *Gutmann und Gutweib*'s piano interlude of bar 5 onwards, the harmonic questions can actually be summed up as the simple ones of major versus minor, and the tonic D versus the pull of its subdominant G. Therefore the decisiveness of the closing gesture on D of bar 12 is not so inappropriate as might at first appear.

This song's harmonic battleground may seem fierce, but in fact it is fought over a closely defined territory. Such a musical impression gets to the heart of Goethe's humorous poetic narrative, for two matter-of-fact statements are made at the beginning of the poem – it is Martinmas, Goodwife loves her husband – and although everything in the poem seems to deny the second statement, this assertion of the marriage relationship sets the tone for everything which follows. Goodwife refuses her husband's command to shut the house door since she is warmly tucked up in bed. She then lets strangers wander unchallenged through the open door and eat the puddings she has baked out of wifely 'love'. If she called out she would lose her wager with Goodman, that whoever speaks first must close the door. In such circumstances the statement of Goodwife's love must seem highly ironic; she is involved in a bitter power struggle, where even the love-gift of baking the puddings exacts its price since Goodwife is now too tired to close the door. The pairing of the couple's names and the poem's relentless matching of metre and rhyme emphasises the tightness of the battle between them, though it is the wife who seems most aware of the game. The husband purports to control the marriage but, as the outcome of the wager reveals, his identity is not so invested in the marital struggle. When the strangers move on from eating the puddings to drinking the husband's schnapps, his outrage betokens a love which transcends the battle with his partner. He would clearly risk all to defend his schnapps, a symbol of his masculine freedom and independence. He loses the wager and his wife demands he close the door. The woman is triumphant, but she can only exert such control within the marriage relationship; the 'love-bond' of the marriage is her only currency of power and she has to play it for all it is worth.

Wolf manages to convey both the claustrophobia of the contest between husband and wife and the seriousness with which it is invested from the woman's point of view.

Example 5.2   Wolf, *Gutmann und Gutweib* (bars 13–31)

Example 5.2 (*cont.*)

The more relaxed narrative styles which depict the scenes of the couple lying down to sleep and later of the strangers passing by their house contrast with the immediate intensity of the song's opening section and suggest a more neutral passing of time while one waits for the next stage in the emotional action. The motivic sequences depicting 'sleep' from bar 13 are much looser in texture than those of the preceding section, a looseness which extends harmonically to a passing cadence to B major in bar 21 (see Example 5.2). Yet rhythmically the phrases soon begin to tighten ominously and the emphatic gestures of bar 21 are exploited fully by the wife in her response from bars 22 to 29, while harmonically the whole section is pulled round to focus on G, the subdominant in the original opposition with D. The passing comment from the husband in bars 20 and 21 becomes drawn into the central battleground, the B major being linked to G and D as in the song's opening phrase. The neutral 'sleep' material which returns from bar 30 offers little prospect of distraction in such a context. The G of bar 29 becomes picked up as a linking thread to bar 38 and the varied return at this point of the section from bar 13.

An unexpected cadence on F♯ major, held from bars 46 to 51 as the close of this repeated section, poses a provocative challenge to the song's growing sense of tonal directedness, but the effect of this shift is immediately contradicted by the emphasis on D minor at the beginning of the song's next episode. The strangers have arrived, and with them comes some newly straightforward march-like material (see Example 5.3). The tonal continuity of this episode with the rest of the song keeps it part of the characters' distinctive battle of wills. D minor oscillates with D major, and the F♯ major which preceded the section and which re-emerges as F♯ minor at bar 65

Example 5.3   Wolf, *Gutmann und Gutweib* (bars 49–68)

Example 5.3 (*cont.*)

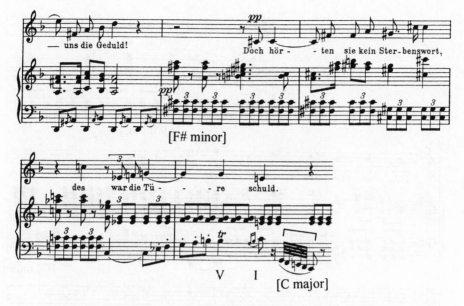

becomes absorbed as part of a quasi-melodic alternation, highlighting the F♯–F♮ opposition within the shift from D major to minor. The overall sense of harmonic direction is confirmed by a subsequent return in bar 70 of the section from bars 5 to 12, though the cadence on D in Example 5.1 is now replaced by one on A. This prepares for a larger-scale arrival on D in bar 82 and balances the song's previous emphasis upon the subdominant.

The ballad is now prepared for the final stage in the marital contest, which begins from bar 82. This is marked by a repetition of the narrative section from bar 52 (see Example 5.3), though the crucial shift to F♯ minor of the previous section is delayed for eight bars by easier side-steps to A♭ and G minor in bars 95 and 96. F♯ minor thus comes in bar 103 as the climax of the section and is held through to a cadence in bar 106 (see Example 5.4). Yet the notion of even a temporary triumph for the husband as he defends his schnapps is dashed by the wife's interjection at bar 107. She subverts the cadence with a return of rhythmic sequences from bar 22, the close on D at bar 115 even more decisive than the one on G in bar 29. The wife's triumphant emphasis upon closure is supported by the postlude's motivic summary of the three contrasting sections of the song. However, it is noticeable that the song's first two-bar question is still not given a straightforward answer in bars 117 and 118. The close in bar 119 comes as an assertion in the face of rising sequences in E♭, rather than as a more simple tonal follow-through. This reawakens the sense of irony that surrounded the original 'answer' of bars 3 and 4. Yet by this point in the song there can no longer be any doubt about the strength of tonal containment. It is now clear that the harmonic areas of E♭ and B♭, as well as the earlier challenge of B and F♯, have been explored and brought within an expansive yet balanced tonal circle around D. The

Example 5.4   Wolf, *Gutmann und Gutweib* (bars 103–29)

precipitate way in which issues of closure and openness are pushed to the forefront of the listener's attention at the beginning of the song heightens the tensions surrounding such tonal processes, so that the woman's triumph over her husband seems almost like an assertion of will, rather than a true emotional test. However, Wolf also makes it clear that the marital struggle is highly significant and the woman has to be allowed to make it real by the energy she invests in it.

Such questions remain humorous in the context of this poem and this song. And one might still ask oneself who gains the greater victory – the woman who wins the wager or the man who holds onto the symbolic power of his schnapps. Yet larger philosophical questions about the nature of our struggles for identity, and the way we use language as part of a game to define ourselves, lie close beneath the surface of this poem, and they too form part of the subject of Wolf's setting.

Goethe's two *Cophtisches Lied* poems address such issues more directly – though here we doubt the success of the speaker in turning the game he embarks upon to his advantage. In *Cophtisches Lied I* the speaker parades his wisdom in finding an answer to the deepest questions that have troubled men through the ages, but the answer he brings seems hardly worth having:

Cophtisches Lied I

Lasset Gelehrte sich zanken und streiten,
Streng und bedächtig die Lehrer auch sein!
Alle die Weisesten aller der Zeiten
Lächeln und winken und stimmen mit ein:
Töricht, auf Bessrung der Toren zu harren!
Kinder der Klugheit, o habet die Narren
Eben zum Narren auch, wie sich's gehört!

Merlin der Alte, im leuchtenden Grabe,
Wo ich als Jüngling gesprochen ihn habe,
Hat mich mit ähnlicher Antwort belehrt:
Töricht, auf Bessrung der Toren zu harren!
Kinder der Klugheit, o habet die Narren
Eben zum Narren auch, wie sie's gehört!

Und auf den Höhen der indischen Lüfte
Und in den Tiefen ägyptischer Grüfte
Hab' ich das heilige Wort nur gehört:
Töricht, auf Bessrung der Toren zu harren!
Kinder der Klugheit, o habet die Narren
Eben zum Narren auch, wie sie's gehört!

[*Coptic Song I*

Let learned men quarrel and dispute,
However austere and ponderous they might be!

All the wisest men of all times
Smile and wink and agree with one another:
It's foolish to wait for fools to improve!
Children of wisdom, leave fools
To their folly, where they belong!

Old Merlin, in his luminous tomb,
When I spoke to him as a youth,
Taught me with the same answer:
It's foolish to wait for fools to improve!
Children of wisdom, leave fools
To their folly, where they belong!

And on the airy heights of India
And in the deep tombs of Egypt
I have only heard the same sacred words:
It's foolish to wait for fools to improve!
Children of wisdom, leave fools
To their folly, where they belong!]

One is not surprised to learn that Goethe conceived this poem as a satirical characterisation of his contemporary, the charlatan magician Alessandro Cagliostro.[20] Yet having exposed the speaker's folly, Goethe uses the clarity of the poetic characterisation to catch at something universal which is communicated by the speaker, though not in the manner he intended. Watching men in their folly and considering its causes can offer up a picture of wisdom – despite what the speaker advises in the refrain of his poem. For the actions of a fool confirm that everything we do is decisive, showing up who we are. And though the speaker may think he is in control of his own fate, he too is tested and exposed by his external circumstances. Understanding the nature of that test might be the beginning of wisdom; so although we do not learn wisdom from following the speaker's direct message, we do from observing him.

Wolf manages successfully to capture the three levels of communication in Goethe's poem, with a manipulation of formal shapes and processes that matches the poet's clarity and subtlety. In his setting of *Cophtisches Lied I* the immediate contrast between the rhythmic security of the song's periodic phrasing and prominent refrain, and the wide range of harmonic and tonal colours, convey the speaker's confidence in capturing the answer to life's greatest mysteries. The semitonal inflexion from E♭ to E♮ or F♭ which helps establish the rhythmic and harmonic impetus of the song in the first bar is highlighted as a potential harmonic gulf in the opening bars of the refrain, bars 9 to 12, and then bridged triumphantly in the ensuing cadence from bars 12 to 14 (see Example 5.5).

However, it is also quickly apparent that this harmonic distance is more assumed than real. The registral leaps in bars 9 to 12, exaggerated by the piano in bars 15 to 17, are clearly part of an elaborate dressing-up when compared with the more dis-

Example 5.5   Wolf, *Cophtisches Lied I*

[20]

Mer - lin der Al - te im leuch-ten-den Gra - be,

pp

Ab major

wo ich als Jüng - ling ge - spro-chen ihn ha - be, hat mich mit ähn - li - cher

E major

[Refrain]

Ant-wort be-lehrt: Tö-richt, auf Beß-rung der To - ren zu har-ren!

pp   *mf*

[F7]   C7 [→ F]

Example 5.5 (*cont.*)

creet semitonal voice-leading in the piano from bars 1 to 7. This introduces three chromatic ascents and descents between E♭ and F, confirming that E♮ can be integrated either as a melodic approach to F, or as a semitonal preparation for the dominant E♭. The only element of uncertainty is the timing of these melodically traced arches against the song's two- and four-bar phrases. For the prominent rhythmic division in bar 4 coincides with E♮, interrupting the flow of its descent back to E♭ for bar 5. Thus while the degree of melodic repetition suggests the speaker is making a fuss about nothing in his refrain, his pretentious phrasing has actually precipitated a moment of harmonic tension on a larger scale. The shift to C major in bar 4 is not entirely answered by the return to A♭ in bar 5, or by the refrain from bar 9. The melodic voice-leading has already suggested that C can be integrated as the dominant of F minor, one of the keys most closely related to A♭, but one has to wait for the refrain of the second verse from bar 25 before this relationship is spelled out. There the refrain's dominant preparation is transposed from A♭ to F, and the C^7 of bar 29 is swiftly redirected to A♭ in bars 30 and 31 to confirm the ease of such substitutions between relative minor and major keys.

There is thus a sense in which Wolf skilfully balances the over-familiarity of the refrain in this song with underlying tensions that do require addressing in some definite fashion. This becomes even more obvious from the relation of the second verse to the refrain of the third. The second verse stresses the melodic ascent from E♭, with the step from D♯ to E being repeated from bars 21 and 22 to 23. Although the further ascent to F is marked in bar 24, there is no corresponding descent back through E to E♭ as in the song's first verse. Instead the articulation of the four-bar phrase outlines a cadence on E major in bar 23. This has to wait for its moment of assimilation. The D♯ to E step of the second verse is recapitulated in a particularly disjunct harmonic phrase from bars 40 to 41, where the rhythmic patterns might seem the only guarantee of continuity. The goal of the voice-leading descent in bar 43 appears as D♯ within B^7, the dominant of E, thus casting E not E♭ as the immediate focus of the chromatic movements. This is confirmed in the short term by the return of the refrain in bar 44 transposed to E. However, the familiarity of the refrain helps trigger the longer-term connection of E with the F♭ of its first statement in A♭, preparing the ear for the sideways move to E♭^{7} in bar 47. The piano's confident repetition in A♭ follows from bar 50, as it did after the song's second verse, though the assertion of the F♭ link to the dominant E♭ now has an added punch.

Therefore, from this song's perversely emphatic language, connections emerge which might not have done so otherwise. The speaker boasts of his control and then one ironically observes that the musical setting of his refrain is either ahead of the material of the verse or struggling to keep abreast of it. On the surface the relationship between verse and refrain never moves as smoothly as one feels it should and one doubts the speaker knows what he is talking about; there are greater mysteries in creation than the superficial ones that he brags of solving. Yet it is also clear from Wolf's setting that our sense of such underlying greater mysteries would not have been awakened without the speaker embarking on his pretentious efforts at definition.

In the second *Cophtisches Lied* setting, Wolf goes perhaps further than Goethe in exposing the pretentiousness of the speaker, using motivic material from the previous song's refrain to point up the two poems' linked world-view. Once more the dressing up of the cadential resolution provocatively exceeds what is warranted by the song's moments of harmonic uncertainty. Goethe prepared the sixth line of his poem as a point of arrival, the 'sinken' picking up the rhyme from 'Winken' in the first line, as well as marking the beginning of the speaker's simple list of life's alternatives. From here the poetic scheme resolves into straightforward rhyming couplets, pushing to the conclusive last line which pulls the poem together by rhyming with the third and fifth lines:

Cophtisches Lied II

Geh! gehorche meinen Winken,
Nutze deine jungen Tage,
Lerne zeitig klüger sein.
Auf des Glückes grosser Wage
Steht die Zunge selten ein;
Du musst steigen oder sinken,
Du musst herrschen und gewinnen,
Oder dienen und verlieren,
Leiden oder triumphieren,
Ambos oder Hammer sein.

[*Coptic song II*

Go! obey my directions,
Make use of your young days,
Learn wisdom in good time.
On the great balance of Fortune
The pointer seldom rests.
You must rise or fall,
You must conquer and win,
Or submit and lose,
Suffer or triumph,
Be the anvil or the hammer.]

Wolf marks Goethe's formal emphasis upon the sixth line of the poem with a complete change of style, so that one feels one has almost moved into a different song. The march-like definition of the two-bar phrases is used to help propel the harmonies to the tonic D, in a relentless stepwise movement which climaxes in the bass's final descent F♯–E–D (see Example 5.6).

In bar 20, F♯ is toyed with as an intermediate harmonic goal that might suggest a directing to B minor. However, the melodic emphasis on C♯'s resolution to D in bars 22

Example 5.6   Wolf, *Cophtisches Lied II*

to 24 and the leading of F♯ via G and G♯ to A in bars 24 and 25 confirm the nature of the song's tonal orientation. The harmonic correction of the voice's A♯ of bar 20 as a B♭ within a strongly marked German sixth in D in bar 24 seems hardly necessary in this context, even if one takes account of the harmonic vagaries of the song's first half. These are not as chaotic as they first appear, although the speaker clearly enjoys exaggerating the uncertainty of each harmonic step. The hestitant vocal declamation and ponderous piano minims of the first section mask the fact that there is an underlying regularity of two-bar phrasing. And the chromatic inflexions from D to D♯ in bar 2, to E♯ in bar 4, far from being random, actually follow a pattern of scalic ascent to F♯ in bar 6. Such melodic inflexions also link into an implied tonal ascent from D to E minor to F♯ minor in the song's first five bars. As in the second section and the F♯ major triad of bar 20, F♯ – outlined melodically by the switch of register at the beginning of bar 6 – marks the limit of such movements from D. The new stepwise ascent from D as outlined in the bass from bar 6 is directed to F♮ not F♯, and the implied keys of F minor from bar 9 and E minor from bar 13 suggest an answering pattern of tonal descent back towards D.

One realises that this song's first section is more contained than might at first appear, an impression that adds to the incongruity of the second section's overly decisive manner. The speaker makes an exaggerated claim about the uncertainty of fortune, so that he can exaggerate the strength of his solution in like manner. He makes it seem that any triumph over fate has to be imposed by force of will or personality, whereas it is clear that the potential for control is there hidden within the questions that present themselves to him; we can see it even if he cannot. It is vision rather than action pure and simple that allows a man to triumph over his circumstances: such is the wiser perception that again emerges from Wolf's setting of the speaker's blunt-edged proposals.

In the famous Harper songs from *Wilhelm Meisters Lehrjahre* Goethe brought his distancing techniques right into the heart of the lyric, creating layers of perception that can hardly be disentangled, and that coalesce at various points into an outpouring of anguish even while they bear the signs of the most considered reflection. In the novel Goethe describes how Wilhelm overhears the Harper singing *Wer nie sein Brot* as a 'kind of improvisation', in which he 'kept on repeating a few stanzas, partly singing them and partly reciting them'. The Harper is often prevented by tears from carrying on, and the harp strings 'would sound on their own until the voice joined in again quietly with broken tones'.[21] The lyric that is recorded is Wilhelm's impression of what he hears as he identifies completely with the song as an outlet for his own emotion. Goethe thus describes the closing of the distance between speaker and observer. As the Harper sings *Wer sich der Einsamkeit ergibt*, Wilhelm encourages him to 'behave simply as if I were not here' and to continue to find 'the most agreeable form of acquaintance within your own heart'.[22] Thus when the Harper asks to be left alone in this poem, the circumstances in the novel point up the introspection which has turned his dialogue with his listeners into a conversation within his own haunted imagination. As the next lyric is introduced, *An die Türen will ich schleichen*, it is described as coming from 'an unhappy person who feels that he is quite close to madness'.[23] And the Harper's description of how others will receive him on his wanderings, dwells on his own acts of separation, on how he passes by without responding to the emotion he arouses:

An die Türen

An die Türen will ich schleichen,
Still und sittsam will ich stehn;
Fromme Hand wird Nahrung reichen,
Und ich werde weitergehn.

Jeder wird sich glücklich scheinen,
Wenn mein Bild vor ihm erscheint;
Eine Träne wird er weinen,
Und ich weiss nicht, was er weint.

[*From door to door*

From door to door I will quietly steal,
And stand there silent and humble;
Kind hands will give me food,
Then I shall go on my way.

Each one will feel happy,
When he sees my picture before him;
He will weep a tear,
But I know not why he weeps.]

Wolf placed this poem at the centre of his three Harper settings, as perhaps the clearest picture of the speaker's emotional circumstances. The Harper presents a 'Bild', an image of his future, which he describes with great certainty as though it has already happened. His separation from the people that he meets is overshadowed by the distance he assumes from his own life. The form and tone of his narrative, the impersonal story-teller mode, interacts with the tale being told, or even becomes the story. As in madness, there is no reality beyond the individual's perception. Yet we have to end up agreeing with the speaker's view of the future, even if this is because we know that his separation from others is self-imposed.

Wolf focusses on the simplicity of this conclusion by tracing a surprisingly straightforward strophic structure which is reflected at all levels of the song, despite the falling chromaticism of the opening bars. The circling melodic shape which encloses bars 1 and 2 re-emerges in the voice's balanced arch from G to G of bars 5 to 8; this is reflected on an even larger scale by the second verse's vocal shape from G to G in bars 17 to 24 (see Example 5.7). Rhythmically, these melodic shapes are highlighted as a source of obvious stability. Within the prelude the repetition of the first

Example 5.7   Wolf, *An die Türen*

[verse 2]

Je - der wird sich glück - lich schei - nen, wenn mein Bild ___ vor

cresc. _ _ _ _

[G7]   [C7]

[20]

ihm er - scheint; ei - ne Trä - ne wird er wei - nen,

[C7]

und ich weiss nicht, was er weint. _____

[Refrain]

G7   C7

[?]

[30]

V   I

one-bar unit helps unfold a sense of the song's periodic dimensions, from one to two bars, and then to four as the repeated figure is answered by bars 3 and 4 and drawn to an imperfect cadence.

The song's steadily unfolding rhythmic structure continues through the first verse, as the balanced arms of the voice's initial four-bar phrase are drawn into a bigger eight-bar shape by the cadential adjustments from bars 8 to 9 and the answering cadence on the tonic in bar 12. Once this cadence moves smoothly into the return of the prelude at bar 13, the voice's eight-bar shape appears enclosed within a larger refrain structure, articulating a sixteen-bar period. The F minor conclusion to the refrain in bar 16 might seem to undermine aspects of this embracing phrase-structure. Yet F becomes an important steadying focus in the song's second verse, the lean to the subdominant balancing the effect of the rising chromatic steps of the bass-line from bar 17. It also balances the pull to the dominant in bar 9, helping project the voice's second eight-bar period as an answer to the first despite the wider range of harmonies. The F minor of bar 16 is revealed as a halfway point in the song's overall structure, answered by the return of the refrain in bar 26 and its subsequent closure upon C.

Wolf's setting underlines how the Harper foresees his future unfolding step by step, each step seeming to follow inexorably from the one before and tracing an enclosed circle that always keeps its connection with the beginning. Yet the periodic stability of the song masks a harmonic uncertainty inherent in the first two bars, which should make one question whether the tonal course of the song is actually fixed from the very first step of the Harper's narrative. If one used the trudging crotchet beat as the measure of a 'step', rather than the larger units of bars or phrases, then within the first bar the keys of F and G are implied as strongly as C. This ambiguity is exploited in the F minor cadence insinuated in bar 16 and in the closing path of the refrain, which moves from C as dominant in bar 25 to C as tonic in bar 30 while still retaining a hint that the tonal outcome could have been reversed. The simple form of Wolf's setting holds without much sense of incongruity or irony. But the madness of a mind predisposed to see certain patterns is still reflected in the prominent role Wolf assigns to certain simple rhythmic and melodic shapes, allowing them to influence a harmonic course that one senses might otherwise have developed with greater fluidity.

Taken by itself, such a setting of Goethe's poem seems slightly undeveloped or incomplete. Yet Wolf clearly conceived this song as part of a grouping with the other two Harper lyrics. They in turn articulate the tonal levels of G and F hinted at alongside C in the opening of *An die Türen*; the end of the latter could be seen in retrospect as a dominant preparation for the beginning of *Wer nie sein Brot*, which takes up the melodic circling of C in the context of F minor. The setting of *Wer sich der Einsamkeit ergibt* anticipates *An die Türen* by beginning with a series of marked rhythmic statements and by outlining tonal areas a fifth either side of the tonic G. Yet there is not the same easy relationship between the one-bar figures and the shape of the larger phrase as in *An die Türen*; the prelude's one-bar sequences set up tonally in opposition to each other, suggesting a mind that is pulling in different directions. And looking at the poem, one notes that although the Harper here makes statements about his condition with the characteristic certainty of *An die Türen*, these now contradict one another. The statement of loneliness in the first stanza is set against the assertion that he is not alone in the second. And although the third stanza makes clear that it is pain and sorrow that keep him company, it remains uncertain whether he truly wishes to be free from them or not. Sometimes they assume the image of a lover, sometimes of a vengeful ghost:

Wer sich der Einsamkeit ergibt

Wer sich der Einsamkeit ergibt,
Ach! der ist bald allein;
Ein jeder lebt, ein jeder liebt
Und lässt ihn seiner Pein.

Ja! lasst mich meiner Qual!
Und kann ich nur einmal
Recht einsam sein,
Dann bin ich nicht allein.

Es schleicht ein Liebender lauschend sacht,
Ob seine Freundin allein?
So überschleicht bei Tag und Nacht
Mich Einsamen die Pein,
Mich Einsamen die Qual.
Ach, werd' ich erst einmal
Einsam im Grabe sein,
Da lässt sie mich allein!

[*He who gives himself to solitude*

He who gives himself to solitude,
Ah! he is soon alone;
Others live, others love
And leave him to his pain.

Yes! leave me to my anguish!
And can I but once
Be truly alone,
Then I shall not be lonely.

A lover creeps by softly listening,
Whether his mistress is alone?
So stealing by day and night
Pain comes to my solitude,
Anguish comes to my solitude.

Example 5.8   Wolf, *Wer sich der Einsamkeit ergibt* (bars 1–6)

Ah, when once at last
I am in my lonely grave,
Then they will leave me alone.]

In Wolf's setting of this poem, the twists and turns of the song's fragmentary phrases betray a common core that transcends the contradictions between them. Thus opposing suggestions of G minor, D minor and C minor within bars 1 to 3 are embraced by a repetition of a melodic circling between B♭ and A. An emphasis upon A♭ within the prelude heightens the melodic resolution to A which in its turn directs back to B♭ (see Examples 5.8 and 5.9). The harmonic distances suggested in the prelude are thus related to an obsessive pattern of repetition and return, just as Goethe marks his poem with the monotonous rhymes of 'allein' and 'Pein'. These voice-leading patterns continue to be obvious within the first two verses of the song. The first verse is still based on the harmonic content of the prelude, though without the step towards the dominant of bar 2. Instead C minor predominates from bars 7 to 11, highlighting the effect of being pulled back to A and then B♭ in the cadence from bars 13 to 14. The second verse concentrates by contrast on the step to the dominant in bar 16, in this case defying the melodic circling back to B♭ for the beginning of the next verse.

Wolf's depiction of 'pain' coming to the Harper as a lover coincides with a suggestion that his patterns of experience might assume a new direction. The melodic shifts between A, B♭ and A♭ which occur from bars 20 to 24 become part of a more open chromatic sequence which does not impose any particular hierarchy of closure. The G minor triad which coincides with the piano's melodic arrival on B♭ in bar 24 is subsequently caught up in a semitonal bass-line ascent to bar 27. However, the melodic move to A♭ still acts as a defining boundary in the climax of bars 26 and 27, resolving conspicuously back to A in bar 28 in preparation for the return of the prelude material in bar 30 and again in bar 35. Despite the scale of the harmonic and textural contrasts Wolf introduces into the third verse, such melodic movements prove an unvarying subtext in the song. Superficially Wolf has imposed a ternary design on the poem, linking verses 1 and 2 together and breaking up Goethe's crucial third verse into a contrasting section and return. Yet the melodic subtext provides another story of monotonous repetition; the images the Harper uses may change, but the emotional message remains the same.

Having shown the Harper acquiescing more openly with the unvarying patterns of his experience in *An die Türen*, Wolf in his setting of *Wer nie sein Brot* depicts the speaker struggling finally to confront the reasons for his emotional imprisonment. The Harper believes his pain allows him to gain knowledge of the 'heavenly powers' which direct his fate, 'powers' that Wolf invokes by opening up new harmonic dimensions in this song compared with the other two. The circling melodic movements and patterns of chromatic descent which are familiar from the previous two settings remerge in the prelude of *Wer nie sein Brot*. But the verse's interpretation of the harmonic implications of these patterns seems quite different. The D♭ and B♮ which melodically encircle the dominant C, and the G♭ and E which surround the tonic F within the prelude, are picked up harmonically in a way that seems to defy immediate closure (see Example 5.10). By coinciding with triads of E♭ minor and B minor in bars 6 and 7, the melodic step from F to G♭/F♯ projects the first vocal phrase beyond the articulation of the four-bar period. The melodic return to C at the cadence-point in bar 8 as part of an A♭⁷ is indeed swept aside by the further melodic shift to B in bar 9 and the voice's continuing chromatic descent towards the cadence of bar 11. The E minor triad at the beginning of this second four-bar phrase and the G♭ triad which articulates the cadence-point could be seen as harmonic extensions of the prelude's melodic encircling of F, but there is little to enforce that connection. Instead the return of the prelude at the end of bar 12 comes as an immediate contrast, giving an incongruous impression of tonal directedness after the openness of the imperfect cadence at the beginning of the bar.

The Harper may have reached towards knowledge of eternal powers, but thus far Wolf's setting represents them as being beyond his immediate experience and threatening the song with incoherence. It is ironic to be brought back to a point of return in bar 12 when the harmonic processes of the previous verse remain so obviously incomplete. The piano refrain seems to be following one harmonic circle and the verse another, one whose course cannot be fully defined. The contrast between the two precipitates a crisis in the second verse, since the returning chromatic movements from bar 17 begin to reveal a greater sense of direction than those of the first verse. The melodic G♭s of bar 17 are drawn to a C⁷ in the following bar and then to B♭ minor, a chord within the tonic F minor, in bar 19. This B♭ becomes a firmer basis from which to return to the E♭ minor of bar 6 at the beginning of bar 21. And from this point the second verse continues to pick up the threads of the first, a B/C♭ triad reemerging at the end of bar 21 and E minor at the beginning of bar 22. Such harmonic proximity reveals that B/C♭ can act as a pivot between such apparently diverse harmonic areas. E minor is further assimilated by the diminished seventh connection to F minor for the beginning of bar 23. The G♭ triads of bars 23 and 24 are now clearly approached from the context of the tonic F, the juxtaposition of the Neapolitan triad and the leading-note E in bar 24 confirming that the distance implied by such melodic and harmonic inflexions has now been measured and caught in relation to the tonic.

The climactic return of the refrain at the end of bar 24 is fully appropriate in such a

Example 5.9   Wolf, *Wer sich der Einsamkeit ergibt*

Example 5.9 (*cont.*)

context. The song's two circles have come together in recognition of the Harper's belief that the gods finally use their exalted position to reinforce man's drudgery on earth. The contrast of this moment with the incongruity of the refrain in bar 12 might make one doubt whether the Harper had truly drawn himself up to knowledge of the divine, or only pulled the divine down to the level of his own despair. As in all the Harper settings, the enclosed form raises as many questions as it answers. It is part of the Harper's struggle to communicate the immeasurable which speaks as much as the actual message that he brings – or which becomes inextricable from the message itself.

It might seem extraordinary to claim that the forms of Wolf's Harper lyrics – considered as an abstract play of openness and closure – lead to the heart of the composer's distinctive intentions; most commentators would wish to draw attention to the chromatic intensity of the harmonies themselves. One might view this as the particular consequence of Wolf wishing to match Goethe's power of formal calculation. However, the evidence of the Spanish and Italian songs written shortly afterwards suggests that Wolf continued to relish the challenge of manipulating refrain structures, and ternary or strophic designs, to reveal an unexpected emotional content. It might be difficult to understand why the composer turned from setting Goethe to what Eric Sams has described as 'a series of rather flat lyrics',[24] if one did not take into account his eagerness to exploit the Spanish poems' repetitive verse structures. The Spanish lyrics' obsession with experiences of passion and guilt reinforced the importance of cyclical repetition to their expression, binding their form and content together in immediately obvious ways. Wolf no longer had to seek out the nature of such relationships, as in the Goethe settings just discussed. The similarity of the Spanish poems' structures and of their emotional concerns encouraged the interpreter to begin to focus on the tiny details of poetic style and image, as in the Italian songbook. One starts to gain the picture of Wolf as craftsman, lovingly and meticulously tracing the melodic or harmonic moments which capture the individuality of the speaker, even within common patterns of human behaviour.

However, Wolf's linking of the songs' details and form still made the differences between songs as striking as their similarities, as with the Harper lyrics. The superficial resemblance between *Ach! wie lang die Seele schlummert!* and *Herr, was trägt der Boden hier* for example – both songs representing the gulf that exists between Man in his sinfulness and the glory that awaits him in Christ – is overshadowed by the particular way in which the gulf is bridged in each song. Both settings are presented as a dialogue between contrasting musical textures, linear chromatic sequences alternating with passages of more vertically conceived triadic texture. Yet in *Ach! wie lang* the latter remain unvarying in their secure emphasis upon the tonic E♭ major, so that the focus of the song falls upon perceiving the implications of E♭ within the contrastingly dissonant textures, and appreciating how the harmonic areas of E minor and A minor can be directed to the tonic via the semitonal relationships of B and A to the dominant B♭. The emphasis is thus upon the 'sinner' and how he can be drawn towards Christ.

Example 5.10   Wolf, *Wer nie sein Brot mit Tränen ass*

In *Herr, was trägt der Boden hier*, by contrast, the triadic textures with which Christ answers the 'sinner' continue to reflect the vagaries of the previous chromatic sequences. They extend the sequences' patterns of harmonic descent, and offer cadence-points that carry little stability in themselves and have to be justified by their relationship with the earlier sections of chromatic voice-leading. Thus the emphasis in this song is upon how Christ identifies with the 'sinner', rather than upon the 'sinner' being drawn to Christ – though both processes bring redemption. In terms of their harmonic treatment, the first song suggests an absolute emphasis upon the tonic E♭, while the second draws out E major from the relative process of weighing up different tonal possibilities. Yet both processes bring formal resolution and show detail and whole being embraced by an absolute musical control. The songs' repetitive structures and clearly marked forms have to be seen as Wolf's means of demonstrating that control, not as guarantees of coherence in an otherwise incoherent language.

Having taken up the challenge of matching Goethe's mediation of form and content, Wolf continued to use song-forms provocatively to demonstrate the certainty of his powers of musical articulation. It is always tempting to see a composer's interest in song as a sign of artistic introspection and withdrawal, but Wolf seemed to welcome song as an immediate test of musical coherence – a continuing measure, in a time of uncertainty, of music's power to generate and communicate meaning.

Chapter six

The Wolfian perspective – comparisons with the songs of Strauss and Mahler

꧁꧂

Having looked at some of Wolf's songs in detail, and various aspects of his compositional approach, one begins to appreciate more why critics have been reluctant to embrace the full complexity of the music. For it would mean allowing elements of sceptical enquiry into the heart of lyrical song, where many have treasured thoughts of Wolf's music as a late flowering of Romanticism. The notion of Wolf measuring out a song's melodic and harmonic dimensions so that each moment can be placed precisely in relation to the whole, confirming or denying the processes of formal argument as they unfold, clashes uncomfortably with the image of lyricism inducing moments of pure forgetfulness. To many musicians, such experiences lie at the centre of the Lied as a genre and give it its special relationship with Romanticism. For in sensing the moment one glimpses the sublime, the freedom from rational boundaries of time and place, as surely as within the expanded dimensions of a Beethoven symphony.

Indeed for Wagner it was crucial that the two experiences of time should be seen to work together, the epic being released into an aura of timelessness by relaxing into moments of 'pure lyricism'. As Carl Dahlhaus has observed, the notion of the leitmotif was itself based on a 'suspension of time that flows'.[1] But perhaps as important to the Ring's aspects of transcendence was the placing of the Rhinemaidens' simple melody at the beginning and end of its long narrative, as both a source and goal for all that happened in between. Adorno characterised such a journey as a collapse into the already known; he believed that the music drama was incapable of true emotional progression, but only of sideways movements that added more layers to hide an underlying stasis.[2] It is known that the final pages of Götterdämmerung, and the interweaving of the Rhinemaidens' music with the 'Valhalla' and 'Redemption' motifs, caused Wagner much trouble. And this has come to represent for some the manufactured unity of the Ring, the contrivedness that Wagner had to conceal by appealing to the innate simplicity of the Rhinemaidens' music. Yet from another point of view, such a stasis reflected the essential nature of the Rhinemaidens' melody itself as it first appeared, with its weightless $^6_4$ subdominant harmonies and circling appoggiat-uras. It reflected how such music both flowed and stood still around the A♭ triad, as one savoured the moment of the first melodic appoggiatura after the uninflected tex-tures of E♭ triads in the preceding prelude.

In the first scene of *Das Rheingold* the impression of melodic inviolability created by the A♭ triad lasts eight bars, before the larger dimensions of the preceding prelude begin to assert themselves and the harmonic range of the Rhinemaidens' dialogue expands to meet them. Yet such a capturing of a moment of undisturbed lyricism remains vital to the *Ring*'s existence as myth, since in that moment one glimpses the stretches of time, the eternity before Alberich comes to inflict pain and growth upon the cycle with his theft of the Rhinemaidens' gold. The lyricism is held briefly so that it is understood to be somewhat apart from the course of the drama as a whole. It sug-gests a different sense of time – one that cannot be measured in the way the rest of the story unfolds, but part of an ever-present continuum that shines through at special moments. Lyrical song thus becomes associated with a kind of immanence that avoids the usual conflicts of the temporal – of change, development and contrast. With such associations Wagner brings forth an extreme version of the ideals of the early composers of *Lieder im Volkston*, in their wish to arrest the development of Viennese symphonic language, by introducing a timeless simplicity that could reach the hearts of all listeners.

However, one wonders whether for post-Wagnerian composers lyrical song could continue to sustain such heightened associations with the immeasurable or eternal, outside the frame of music drama itself. Edward F. Kravitt has commented upon the fashion for endings that fade away into nothing among late nineteenth-century song-writers – Mahler and Strauss most prominent among them.[3] Yet there is a poignancy in many of their songs that comes from the lyrical moment being revealed for what it is, passing and vulnerable. It is often represented as a door to eternity that one cannot pass through, bringing first and foremost a sense of loss.

In Strauss's much-loved song *Morgen* (Tomorrow) the composer exploits such poignancy to the fullest. The lyrical effect of the added sixth in the second bar sends immediate tremors through the song's harmonic fabric, as seen in the lean towards A minor in bar 3 and then towards E minor in bars 5 and 6. And yet the melodic arches of two and four-bar phrases proceed undisturbed to the cadential gesture of bar 15 (see Example 6.1). Strauss articulates in this way the ambiguity of the added sixth itself, which pulls away from the tonic triad but is also connected with it as a barely separate harmonic entity. The melodic rise to E and its completion to G in the song's second bar sums up a harmonic movement that is arrested before it can happen, a movement that remains poised on the brink of actuality.

The course of the whole song is known in this moment, as a continued suspension of harmonic distances. The rise and fall of the unbroken statement of the tonic in Example 6.1 is repeated to the hushed commentary of the voice as the main body of the song. It is not even disturbed by the harmonic side-steps of the song's epilogue

Example 6.1   Strauss, *Morgen* (bars 1–16)

from bar 31, for the tritonal steps from B^7 to F^7 are treated in the same revolving fashion as the added sixth of the opening. Indeed the harmonically implied chain of thirds at the close – the A♭ triad in bar 36 comes to fill the third between the B^7 and F^7 of bars 33 to 35 – links back to the melodic thirds of bars 1 and 2. The D triad of bar 37 completes the chain and allows the first phrase to slip in as a peaceful summary, confirming the song's unbroken mood (see Example 6.2). Nothing in the course of this song brings one nearer to resolving the poignant tension of its added sixth – once it has been stated it is as if there is nothing more to be done or said. Indeed in listening to this song one almost holds one's breath, fearing its particular sense of suspension might be lost and with it the whole fabric of the song. The vision of 'tomorrow' shimmers before the eyes of the speaker, but one knows that no claim can be made upon it; though it remains near it is always out of reach.

In this song Strauss managed to make a sense of transience almost palpable, but he also diminished the workings of time in a way that was in danger of negating lyrical expression altogether. For if there is no past or future to ward off, no unfolding of events to hold back momentarily, then the sense of the present moment loses its hold

Example 6.2   Strauss, *Morgen* (bars 31–42)

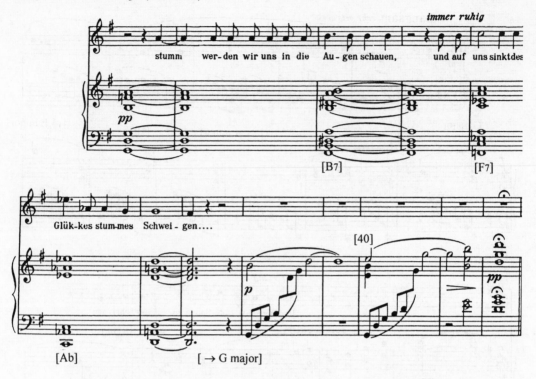

upon the imagination as an entry to eternity, and becomes almost a bleak 'no-man's land'. Mahler realised this contradiction perhaps more clearly than Strauss, and allowed poetic and musical images of loss to permeate even his most tranquil songs. In Rückert's *Ich bin der Welt abhanden gekommen* (I am lost to the world) the poet gains his view of heaven only by relinquishing all hope for himself on earth; he lives only through song. The resolutions to conflict that he finds in 'song' carry no weight for the rest of human existence – to enjoy them one has to move into his 'world' apart. In Mahler's musical setting, the balance of rising and falling phrases, which as in *Morgen* weave a sense of calm suspended motion, is shown to emanate from the song's initial oscillation between the pitches of B♭ and C. These two melodic pitches are bound together by their first repetitions against a B♭ pedal, and by their re-emergence at the high-point and close of each phrase. Thus the B♭ that marks the peak of the cor anglais's first contour in bar 5 is accompanied by a B♭ to C movement in the low horn, bringing with it a sense of C minor sonority to colour the phrase expansion with a moment of wistfulness, before the melodic descent back to the opening fragments (see Example 6.3).

The particular colour of the C minor harmony returns at the high-point of each of the song's three verses. The voice's melodic arrival on B♭ in bar 14 is carried beyond C to E♭ by the voice in bar 16, though without escaping the harmonic colour of the sub-mediant. It accompanies the vocal flight to F, the expressive melodic appoggiatura in bar 25 and, most tellingly, returns in bar 32 to cut back the second verse's growing harmonic and textural momentum. The following cadence upon C major at the beginning of bar 38 only serves to emphasise the effect of a fall to C minor in the next bar and the renewed melodic descent for the beginning of the third verse. In the third verse C becomes more pervasive still, both harmonically and melodically, so that there is no longer any sense of opposition between major and minor, the tonic E♭ and C minor. The blurring of the two is summed up in the voice's arrival on '*stillen* Gebiet' (quiet sphere) in bar 46, where the held melodic C is accompanied by simultaneous suggestions of both C minor and A♭ major triads. In the postlude these harmonic and melodic thirds continue to create a sense of space around the tonic, which lingers on in the cor anglais's final C–B♭ appoggiatura (see Example 6.4).

Such an ending offers tantalising hints of continuation, leaving one with the sound of the initial melodic fragment, the seed for further linear and harmonic journeys. And yet one also realises that the journeys already traced have never actually moved beyond the circle suggested by the B♭–C oscillation itself, and perhaps cannot do so. The expansion suggested by the melodic rise from B♭ to C is contradicted by the harmonic effect of the added sixth, and the treatment of C minor as a constant adjunct to the tonic triad. Growth is surrounded by decay, or by a collapse inwards towards closure, so that in one sense the oscillation between B♭ and C remains the song's only substance. Mahler reveals the poet's 'song' in its most vulnerable guise, filling it with impressions of the immeasurable but at the cost of reducing its actual substance to a mere fragment.

Adorno claimed Mahler knew he was facing the irretrievable collapse of musical language, and was seeking to piece together a new one from among 'lost things',[4] from the 'fragments and scraps of memory'.[5] Most of the Mahler literature would seek to put forward personal reasons for this composer's fascination with musical images of death and eternity, and his expression of them in song. The demands of the genre itself are often taken as secondary to the needs of the composer's artistic personality, as though the medium of song might mould itself to any expressive intention. And yet the comparison of *Morgen* and *Ich bin der Welt abhanden gekommen* – a kind of comparison that could be extended through many of Mahler and Strauss's songs – suggests a shared awareness of the particular opportunities of song, the chance to capture a lyrical moment that hints at possibilities for expansion but withdraws from realising them. Underlying such songs lingered a fear that such realisation might not be possible, and that after Wagner one could not presume to 'measure the immeasurable' through lyrical song. In harnessing the ideals of the early Romantic composers of *Lieder im Volkston*, Wagner robbed lyricism of much of its naivety. The immediacy of lyrical expression was devalued or coloured by more complex intentions, and in many ways there was no way for Lieder composers to regain the earlier simplicity.

Taking such a view, it is difficult to blame Wolf for spoiling a straightforward enjoyment of lyrical song. Rather than being wilfully disturbing he was registering, in his

Example 6.3   Mahler, *Ich bin der Welt abhanden gekommen* (bars 1–12)

own fashion, that the time for such straightforwardness had passed. The loss of
simplicity in his songs is more striking than in Strauss's or Mahler's, since he
addresses it in more explicit ways, focusing immediately on questions of continuity or
direction rather than leaving such questions to be implied on the edges of his songs.
And yet Wolf's Lieder still bear witness to the impact of moments of 'pure forgetfulness' – even if that impact is contained within precise formal circumferences. In the
Italian song *Wie viele Zeit verlor ich* (How much time I have lost), the poet regrets that
heaven is now closed to him since he has worshipped his beloved's face rather than
God. Wolf makes the moment of supreme realisation come with the lingering melodic
appoggiatura on 'schön *Veigelein*' (my beautiful little bird) in bar 14, the weightless-
ness of the interrupted cadence in this song evoking memories of Isolde gazing into

the eyes of a sick Tristan and dropping her sword in Wagner's *Tristan und Isolde* (see Example 6.5).

Wagner's musical image, first introduced in bar 17 of *Tristan und Isolde*'s prelude, makes similar play of rising semitonal movement in the bass, set against the unexpected release of the falling tone of the melodic appoggiatura (see Example 6.6). In Example 6.6, this moment of suspension arrests the prelude's progress of rising sequences and draws out a new kind of melodic impulse. In *Wie viele Zeit verlor ich* the melodic and harmonic joining of A♭ and D belongs firmly within the argument of the song as it has unfolded thus far, and brings an answer of definite closure to clash iron-

Example 6.4   Mahler, *Ich bin der Welt abhanden gekommen* (bars 57–67)

ically with the immediate impression of musical suspension. The song's tonal argument revolves throughout around the relationship of E♭ to the tonic G minor. As in *Ich bin der Welt abhanden gekommen*, the submediant functions ambiguously, both pulling away from the dominant and helping to reinforce moments of return and closure. In bars 5 to 8, for example, E♭ partly serves to emphasise the inevitability of the return to D^7 in bar 6, which promises to rhyme with bars 2 and 4 and reinforce the periodic regularity of two-bar phrases. But in the second half of bar 6, E♭ unexpectedly replaces D as the goal of the phrase, and opens the way for a sideways shift to B♭ major in bar 8 for the close of the next two-bar phrase. As the second half of the song unfolds from bar 9, D and E♭ begin to emerge in clear opposition to one another, the tonal goal implied by the D^7 of bars 9 and 10 being set against E♭'s own leading towards A♭ in bar 12. A♭ re-emerges at the moment of expressive climax in bar 14, but the voice's replacement of D♭ with D♮ at this point now removes any illusion of E♭ bringing escape from the pull of the tonic G minor. In bar 15, and again in the penultimate bar of the song, E♭^{7} is respelled as a German sixth in G minor, confirming its subordination to D in the preparation for a final cadence.

The immediate poignancy of this song's climax remains intact, but the impression of momentary suspension is subordinated to its message in relation to the whole – which is one of tonal closure. As the singer lingers *nachlassend* over the poet's naming of his beloved, Wolf suggests how the image of her face spreads to fill his mind. But the consequences of such worship – the closed doors of heaven – are shown to be more important still. The song's moment of expressive summary is allowed to pass on and be overtaken by the effect of the final relentless steps to closure.

Even in a song such as Wolf's setting of Mörike's *Auf einer Wanderung* (On a Walking Tour), which breathes a more carefree spirit of Romanticism, the composer prepares for its central moment of lyrical release and binds it carefully into the structure of the whole. The poem is all about a moment of rapture when the traveller loses all sense of time and place and the 'Muse' possesses him:

Auf einer Wanderung

In ein freundliches Städtchen tret ich ein,
In den Strassen liegt roter Abendschein.
Aus einem offnen Fenster eben,
Über den reichsten Blumenflor
Hinweg, hört man Goldglockentöne schweben,
Und eine Stimme scheint ein Nachtigallenchor,
Dass die Blüten beben,
Dass die Lüfte leben,
Dass in höherem Rot die Rosen leuchten vor.

Lang hielt ich staunend, lustbeklommen,
Wie ich hinaus vors Tor gekommen,
Ich weiss es wahrlich selber nicht.

Example 6.5   Wolf, *Wie viele Zeit verlor ich*

Example 6.6   Wagner, Prelude to Act I of *Tristan und Isolde* (bars 15–18)

Ach hier, wie liegt die Welt so licht!
Der Himmel wogt in purpurnem Gewühle,
Rückwärts die Stadt in goldnem Rauch;
Wie rauscht der Erlenbach, wie rauscht im Grund der Mühle!
Ich bin wie trunken, irr'geführt –
O Muse, du hast mein Herz berührt
Mit einem Liebeshauch!

[*On a Walking Tour*

I enter into a friendly little town,
In the streets lies a red evening light.
Just then from an open window,
Over the richest pile of flowers
One hears golden-voiced bells floating,
And one voice sounds like a chorus of nightingales,
So that the blossoms tremble,
So that the air quickens,
So that the roses gleam a brighter red.

I stood long in astonishment, held by rapture.
How I arrived in front of the town gate,
I truly do not know myself.
Ah here, how brightly the world appears!
The sky is woven in crowds of purple,
Behind me lies the town in a golden haze;
How the stream ripples in the alders, how the mill rumbles below!
I am as if drunk, confused –
Oh Muse, you have stirred my heart
With a breath of love!]

Yet in his setting Wolf draws out the stages that lead to the poet's moment of ecstasy, as though inspiration might be captured as part of a rational process.

In the first stage of his emotional journey the poet is shown to be mostly engrossed in the rhythms of walking, even though chromatic inflexions convey his feelings of suppressed excitement (see Example 6.7). This excitement spills over in bar 9 as the B♮ upbeats of the first six bars usher in a shift of tonal level, from E♭ to B/C♭ major. Already the poet's eyes are being drawn away from his path to the sights around him,

Example 6.7   Wolf, *Auf einer Wanderung*

Example 6.7 (*cont.*)

Db major

[20]

C major

E major

[30]

[Eb7]   [Ab7]

Example 6.7 (*cont.*)

Example 6.7 (*cont.*)

the further shift to D major in bar 13 bringing in a series of semitonal side-steps – to D♭ in bar 17 and C in bar 21. The rhythmic momentum of the piano motif also slows from bar 13 and the voice begins to slip out of time with the piano's phrases. With the poetic enjambment from the fourth to the fifth line of the first stanza, the voice spills over the four-bar division from bar 16 to bar 17. The poet's steps are shown to become more haphazard still as the piano too deserts the four-bar phrase for an unexpected shift from C to E major in bar 23. The previous semitonal chain is broken, leaving little sense of how this tonal level is to be connected with the tonic E♭, while rhythmically the motivic fabric dissolves into one-bar units.

The E♭ pedal of bar 27 recentres the song harmonically and suggests the poet trying to pull together all his wandering impressions. The texture shifts decisively from the motion of walking to a series of impassioned chromatic sequences that demand some kind of immediate goal. However, the directional movement of the texture is not yet matched by a clear sense of tonal resolution. The flatward impulse of the E♭7 and A♭7 in bars 27 to 30 continues the harmonic tendency of much of the song's first section, and suggests a mind still struggling to express the many sensations it has experienced. The cadence upon E♭ in bar 34 sets up a harmonic landmark – as though Wolf were establishing a measure of consciousness – but it fails as yet to draw the song into one course. The subsequent return to E♭7 and the bass-line oscillations between E♭ and F♭/E confirm that the conflicting tonal movements have still to be absorbed into a clear circle around the tonic key.

The walking motions of the song's first section begin again without the poet having balanced the internal with the external, his feelings with his impressions. And yet the return of the steady succession of rhythmic sequences from bar 50 onwards actually throws up a new kind of harmonic chain, which begins to help chart the song's tonal space. The continuing descent by fifths from G7 and C7 in bars 50 to 52, to F in bar 53, helps orientate the voice's next four-bar phrase, preparing for the crucial moment of arrival on B♭ in bar 63. The mediant shift to A major in bar 59 suggests there is still a drift in the poet's thoughts before the moment of homecoming in bar 63 itself. Wolf manages to capture both a feeling of surprise and of all falling into place, as the poet now finds the words for his experience – 'Ach hier, wie liegt die Welt so licht!' (Ah here, how brightly the world appears!). The intensity of the moment in bar 63 is expressed by the motif's new melodic arches, sustained by two-bar repetitions and imitating voices within the piano texture. Even the four-bar shifts of tonal level fail to disturb the sense of lyrical fulfilment, for these follow a new symmetrical pattern of rising thirds which leads back to B♭ in bar 73. Such circling progressions suggest time standing still while the scene is held within the poet's eye. But they also show how the song's most wayward harmonies – the mediant steps as seen in the shifts to E in bar 23 and to A in bar 59 – can be drawn into patterns of resolution. The directional sequences from bar 77 here assume an appropriate air of inevitability as they aim for a triumphant resolution upon E♭ in bar 82. And in one sense bar 82 offers itself as the climax of the song, the moment when containment is confirmed and the poet welcomes the creative spirit which gives meaning to his journey. Yet Wolf also shows how the earlier excitement has inevitably passed into reflection. The augmentation of the motif in bar 82 confirms the lyrical transformation of bar 63, rather than offering a further surprise; just as, harmonically, the goal of E♭ comes as one that has been fully prepared.

The return of the initial version of the song's motif from bar 90 and the echo of its augmented version in bar 102 sustain this mood of reflection and reawaken us to a sense of time that places the moment of ecstasy firmly in the past. Wolf appears to detach himself from the lyrical rapture of the song's central passage, and show the traveller returning to the everyday activity of walking, with only one last look back over his shoulder. However, the passage from bar 63 retains its special effect as first offering the key to the song's balance and resolution. There is little sense that it is undermined by the song's almost prosaic ending; the lyrical moment keeps its power as the turning-point which leads the way to the fulfilment of resolution.

In Wolf's songs the moment of 'pure forgetfulness' is protected by its place within the whole as it unfolds in time, and one does not need to fear the ending of the song as the loss of lyricism's magic. Mahler's perception of such moments of closure was quite different, for while he often prolonged the impression of lyrical rapture and of weightless flight to far greater lengths, he also depicted a sense of loss when such extensions had to come to an end. In 'Ging heut' morgens übers Feld' from *Lieder eines fahrenden Gesellen*, the spinning out of melodic phrases reaches unprecedented dimensions as the composer evokes the traveller's delight in external nature. The continuous interplay between the voice and the instruments almost prevents any one moment from emerging as an expressive summary of the whole, until bar 64 where the change of key to B major suggests a step aside from the previous round of phrases in D major. Here Mahler begins to hold the voice apart from the instruments, allowing its melodic dominant to ring on as the traveller reflects on the world before him – 'Und da fing im Sonnenschein gleich die Welt zu funkeln an' (And in the sunshine the whole world began at once to sparkle) (see Example 6.8). The harmonic openness of this moment is taken up in a further tonal shift to F♯ major from bar 83, drawing out another melodically suspended phrase (see Example 6.9).

Closure in this song might now seem postponed indefinitely, and indeed the composer delays reintroducing the tonic D until the D minor of the following song of the cycle. Yet once individual melodic phrases are isolated from the texture as in Example 6.9, the rhythmic momentum propelling them begins to drain away and their open-endedness begins to seem a source of weakness rather than strength. The simple sequences with which the voice asks 'Nun fängt auch mein Glück wohl an?' (Will my happiness now begin?) seem by themselves too insubstantial to fill the surrounding instrumental textures. And the voice's final augmented descent to the tonic could be interpreted as a reluctant admission of defeat, as much as an expressive hovering over closure. In contrast to the earlier impressions of 'endless melody' Mahler shows the voice seeming to run out of breath, so that the horn, oboe and violin are left to help

Example 6.8   Mahler, 'Ging heut' morgens übers Feld', *Lieder eines fahrenden Gesellen* (bars 64–71)

the voice make the needed resolution. Although the pauses in the song's melodic flow have allowed one to savour the expressivity of the vocal line, they have also brought a poignant dissolution.

Strauss excelled in staving off such physical hints of mortality in his songs, defying the usual limits of breath and contour in his treatment of the voice. In both *In goldener Fülle* (In golden abundance) and *Wie sollten wir geheim sie halten* (How could we have kept it secret) his vocal lines combine melodic simplicity with an almost over-whelming build-up of phrases. Both poems speak of the poets' confidence in love transcending all barriers of time, a confidence that refuses to doubt or question – 'Wir schreiten in goldener Fülle bis an das Ende der Welt' (We walk in golden abundance until the world's end). One might still sense a certain vulnerability in these poems, in

Example 6.9   Mahler, 'Ging heut' morgens übers Feld' (bars 94–9)

their needing to rely on the poet's assertions to close out the possibility of change and decay. In both songs Strauss reinforces the notion that the present can expand to embrace the future, by spinning a piano texture of relentlessly pulsing triplet rhythms, and one wonders how the voice would support its flight if this rhythmic texture were withdrawn. Yet with at least one of his songs – 'Beim Schlafengehen' (While falling asleep) from the *Vier letzte Lieder* – Strauss faced this challenge, removing a regular rhythmic impetus from the song's instrumental textures, leaving the voice more vulnerable as it sought to continue its melodically unbroken journey towards 'eternity'. The line holds triumphantly even with the orchestral colours shifting all around it, and though at times in danger of appearing thin and disembodied, the voice seems to succeed in passing beyond the usual tensions and limitations of song.

One might wish to say the same for the lyricism of Mahler's last song from *Das Lied von der Erde* – the voice's melodic lingering on the supertonic at the close of 'Abschied' being understood not merely as the effective suspension of closure, but as the natural-seeming answer to the work's particular balance of symphony and song. This manner of closing – where the final melodic resting on the mediant of the violins seems to blend as an echo of the voice's fragment rather than offering external completion – also answers the earlier antagonism between lyrical flight and closure as seen so clearly in Mahler's *Lieder eines fahrenden Gesellen*. In the final song of the cycle, 'Die zwei blauen Augen', the expanding transformation of the vocal line as it reaches F major – indicating the poet's rest under the linden tree – is effectively denied by the flute's cadential fragments, imposing a close on F minor.

Such messages of reluctant closure, as seen in the final song of *Lieder eines fahrenden Gesellen* and in 'Ging heut' morgens', are challenged by Mahler's First Symphony. The first movement of the symphony takes up the song-material of 'Ging heut' morgens' exactly at the point in the third verse where it was poised over a new harmonic and textural openness, as though in a symphonic context there need be no fears of lyrical dissolution. The notion of 'running out of breath' is confronted at the end of the first stage of the symphonic exposition of the song-material, in a return at figure 12 to the large-scale suspended textures of the slow introduction. And the symphonic answers begin to emerge in the development of the cellos' sighing fragment at this point into an increasingly powerful march figure, one which adds new dimensions to the movement's spinning out of song phrases. The potential of these dimensions becomes fully apparent in the finale, where the questions surrounding 'Ging heut' morgens' are absorbed into a much larger symphonic narrative. However, the unexpected unleashing of dramatic energy which marks the beginning of the finale appears as a response to the particular crisis of the third movement – and this again revolves around song. For as part of its oddly assorted chain of funeral march figures, the third movement introduces material from 'Die zwei blauen Augen', again selecting its most expansive episode, the final stanza in the major. The effect here of the flute's cadential fragments in the minor is reinforced by a symphonic return to the leaden phrases of the 'Frère Jacques' march, as though symphony were perversely to be pulled into the same restrictive pattern of closure as song.

The First Symphony's finale gives the lie to such fears, though the vehemence of its style and the convoluted repetitions of its form reveal they are not to be dismissed easily. And indeed the stylistic and formal confrontation between song and symphony which marks the rest of Mahler's output continues to echo the tension between lyrical flight and closure, as grasped so clearly and poignantly in the songs themselves. The evidence is unclear about exactly how much the conception of *Lieder eines fahrenden Gesellen* became interwoven with that of the First Symphony itself.[6] However, if song provided the source and focus for Mahler's distinctive crises of expression, then symphony assumed much of the weight of finding answers to them. Even in *Das Lied von der Erde* the sense of fulfilment surrounding the voice's special moment of 'open-ended closure', relies upon the motivic identity of the melodic 3–2 (E–D) fragment on 'ewig', balanced against the rising 5–6 (G–A) of the flute, and this motif's relationship to the processes of symphonic development underlying the work as a whole. These major second intervals first emerge from a complex of fourths at the opening of *Das Lied von der Erde* (E–A–D–G), fourths which define both the melodic and harmonic aspects of the opening song, 'Das Trinklied von Jammer der Erde'. As fourths, these motivic pitches are articulated as striving upbeats, suggesting a search for rhythmic and tonal definition. Yet even here there are hints of such pitches being drawn together as part of a more unified grouping, as a pentatonic scale on C

(C–D–E–G–A). The last song's motivic emphasis upon the intervals of a second high-lights this contrasting characterisation, so that in the closing bars of 'Abschied' the motivic pitches are able to be resolved without conflict into the single entity of an added sixth chord on C – a sonority which the voice suggests might expand to absorb the supertonic D as much as the submediant A.

The symphonic aspects of this resolution prevent it from appearing as a retreat into lyrical stasis in the manner of *Ich bin der Welt abhanden gekommen* or Strauss's *Morgen*. And as though to confirm his release from such restrictions, Mahler went on to develop the rising and falling motifs of 'Abschied' (the melodic 3–2 and 5–6 move-ments) as the basis for his Ninth Symphony. Like Strauss in his *Vier letzte Lieder*, Mahler was led by his involvement with song to seek an expression which tran-scended its limits; song was a measure, but one that the composer seemed to wish to show he could finally leave behind.

The *Vier letzte Lieder* and *Das Lied von der Erde* are held as two of the most important landmarks of late Romanticism, summing up the sense of loss that continued to pervade music after Wagner, yet also the composers' determination, as the critic Max Graf described it, to ride on to new dawns.[7] Wolf's final completed work might seem limited in such company, for his three *Michelangelo-Lieder* remain firmly lodged within the confines of song and promise little distraction from the references to mortality that pervade the poems themselves.

In the first song, 'Wohl denk' ich oft' (I often ponder), Wolf picks up the poet's retro-spective tone as he reviews the course of his life from a point now well removed from his earlier struggles. The poem ends in an assertion of the artist's present love and fame, but there is no clue as to how he reached such an exalted position nor any reliv-ing of his path to glory. The past and the present are stated side by side, with a barrier between them that Wolf highlights by an unexpected harmonic shift in bar 15 – from the prevailing tonality of G minor to a triad of E major (see Example 6.10). Such a harmonic and textural lurch might be thought to break the song apart; but in fact it is surprising how swiftly Wolf is able to move from such a point of disjuncture to final closure on G. The effect of the E is still registered in the voice's protracted melodic climax on E of bar 18, and the unexpected deflection to the subdominant in bars 19 and 20 which also allows the melodic E to ring on. But these steps are easily assimi-lated as effective ways of stressing the overall change of mode from G minor to G major, rather than suggesting harmonic tensions demanding further resolution. Similarly the chromatic inflexions within the song's first fourteen bars – like the passing cadence to A♭ in bar 9 – serve to emphasise the minor mode rather than pulling away from the song's periodic returns to the dominant or tonic. The lean towards the subdominant in bars 13 and 14 brings the first hint of any alternative tonal goal, a hint that is overtaken by the dramatic interruption of the shift to E major itself. For at this moment it is as though a door were opened from within the closed round of retrospection, promising new horizons. Yet though the song's subsequent change to the major does create a sharp sense of contrast, the overall message of closure remains unchanged; the 'round' continues, reflecting the solidity of the tonal frame that has already been established. The future might appear to bring 'transcendence', but Wolf is more concerned to show how the contrast it brings works against the circumference of the poet's life as a thing already known.

Such patterns reemerge in the following two songs of the *Michelangelo-Lieder*, though with very different effect. The second song, 'Alles endet, was entstehet' (Everything that lives must die) suggests a collapse of any expectation of change or expansive development. For all its poignant chromaticism, the song remains closely guarded within the rise and fall of four-bar phrase-structures and the pull of C♯minor or its relative key, E major. The surprise perhaps is that stylistic material that appears on the surface so Wagnerian can remain so closed and song-like. The way in which *Tristan*esque sequences – as in the setting of the line 'Denken, Reden, Schmerz und Wonne' (Thinking, speaking, sorrow and joy) – close back upon themselves within a persistent dominant preparation for E suggests both the extent of Wolf's control of Wagnerian language and his identification with the immediate formal boundaries of song.

In the third song, 'Fühlt meine Seele das ersehnte Licht vom Gott' (Does my spirit sense the longed-for heavenly light), Wolf does begin to present such enclosure of rhythmic phrase and tonality as an imprisonment. The tightening repetition of one-bar units within the four-bar period, as seen in the piano prelude, creates an urge to expansion which is immediately reflected in the broader sweep of the first vocal phrase, carrying it forward from bar 5 to bar 11 without pause (see Example 6.11). Harmonically, the first vocal phrase remains close to the tonic E minor, while the motivic outline of bar 5 supports the voice and piano's melodic extensions at almost every point. However, there is an expectation of change which projects the melodic contour towards the moment of arrival in bar 12, the harmonic shift to E major and the new crystallisation of the voice's motif from bar 5.

Wolf shows the poet seeking to focus his mind and identify the vision or sensation that draws him on; but with each effort the moment of lyrical realisation only seems to slip further from his grasp. For the new rhythmic definition of bar 12 only serves to intensify the song's forward momentum, as rising sequences from bars 12 to 17 – and then again from bars 19 to 21 and bars 23 to 25 – create a newly persistent series of wave-like movements. The intermediate pauses underline the intensity of these questioning gestures, but also raise the fear that they may be beyond answering. The extreme registral collapse from bar 27 to bar 30, and the subsequent return to the subdued textures of the song's first vocal phrase, suggest that the poet's aspirations only lead to despair. Like Mahler, Wolf here seems to lament the closing in of formal boundaries, as the song moves towards closure without fulfilling the expectations of its urgent melodic and rhythmic expansions. The melodic contours which emerge from bar 31 are on a significantly smaller scale than the melodic flight from bar 5, fitting easily within the framework of a four-bar phrase.

One is surprised that such half-stifled echoes are still succeeded in bar 36 by a

Example 6.10   Wolf, 'Wohl denk' ich oft', *Michelangelo Lieder*

Example 6.11   Wolf, 'Fühlt meine Seele', *Michelangelo Lieder*

E major

Example 6.11 (*cont.*)

[Return]

[30] *Im Hauptzeitmass (wie zu Anfang).*

E minor

E major

[40]

I⁶₄   VI   IV   II7   V7   I

switch to the major mode and a series of heightened motivic repetitions, as at bar 12. One might imagine that the song had withdrawn from all hints of continuing expansion. However, such material as appears at bar 36 was always ambiguous in its import, and with the present shift of context Wolf allows its lyrical aspect – the dwelling in the moment – to preside over any more directional impulses. The effect of the motivic repetitions now centres attention on E major as a point of return, rather than creating impetus for further expansions. As the voice and piano continue to balance melodically around the dominant B, the song dwindles in perspective from seeming to seek answers in some musically uncharted space beyond the build-up of motivic phrases, to finding space within the phrases near at hand. The semitonal oscillations between B and B♭/A♯ and between C and C♯ convey a greater sense of harmonic movement in the section from bar 36 than in the melodically more diffuse section from bar 12. And Wolf shows such inflexions continuing past the simple cadential statement of bars 40 and 41, into the postlude's closing summary.

In the section from bar 36 the song's poetic focus finally emerges – the poet finds the object of his yearning by gazing into the eyes of his beloved. The answer is so simple, it comes dangerously near to being an anticlimax. Yet eyes that can prompt such a tortured narrative must exert a strange power; they uncover the poet's readiness for introspection, his eagerness to turn the simplest longing – the longing for love – into a journey of self-discovery. In Wolf's song, as in Michelangelo's poem, this inner journey almost overbalances any possibility of the song resolving into a simple lover's conceit. One wonders whether such a conventional solution is not self-imposed, as a final counsel of despair – an ironic withdrawal from the *Tristan*esque challenge of searching for the inexpressible. Yet Wolf gives us signs that such a conventional context has been present from the outset. The summary of the postlude highlights the motivic repetitions which have crystallised each stage in the poet's journey, even while urging him forward to the next step of discovery. The 'inner journey' and its overriding context cannot be divorced from one another; in Wolf's song this is the false illusion that sends the poet chasing off towards a meaningless vacuum. Wolf shows the beloved's face keeping its hold upon the poet's imagination as the object that both provokes and contains the force of his longing – there is no 'beyond' that has not been generated by his immediate response to her eyes.

As in *Wie viele Zeit verlor ich*, Wolf lays bare the poet's human mortality and with it the constraints upon his emotional expression, seeing them with his objective songwriter's eye. Even with such an impassioned song as 'Fühlt meine Seele', Wolf continued to treat song as a tool of objectivity. And yet the mystery of what remains unsaid haunts this song, as powerfully as Mahler's 'Abschied' or Strauss's 'Beim Schlafengehen'. The crucial difference lies in how or where one senses it. For instead of drawing one towards an indefinite continuation, with a journey always pointing beyond the boundaries of song, Wolf revealed the mystery within the circle of song-like containment itself. By concentrating on his songs' movement to closure, Wolf captured the lyrical moment as it turned from something present to something past, or from potential to realisation, without allowing our sense of one to shut out a sense of the other. In uncovering the impact of the lyrical moment as it moved into the past Wolf might be said to have stressed the sense of loss that Mahler and Strauss only hinted at. And yet the knowledge of how such a moment affects a song as a whole lasts longer than the echoes of the lyrical moment itself, and it was this knowledge that Wolf offered so powerfully in his music. He captured the effect of lyricism in a way that brought a new sense of expressive inviolability to song, even if he recognised he could not recover the old. He could not reverse the stylistic associations of his time or insulate himself from the tensions of the post-Wagnerian era. But, in his songs, Wolf articulated ways of finding a creative balance in the midst of flux, of remaining artistically true to the moment and its consequences, that speak beyond his time and should encourage us in our new evaluations of his music and of song.

Notes

❦

Introduction

1. See Ernst Decsey, *Hugo Wolf*, 4 vols. (Berlin and Leipzig, 1903–6), vol. I, p. 57: 'As a compass always points to the north, Wolf's thinking and feeling always stuck in the Wagnerian "direction".'
2. Hugo Wolf-Verein in Wien, ed., *Gesammelte Aufsätze über Hugo Wolf*, 2 vols. (Berlin, 1898), vol. I, p. xi.
3. See Thomas Leibnitz, 'Josef Schalk: ein Wagnerianer zwischen Anton Bruckner und Hugo Wolf', *Bruckner Jahrbuch 1980* (Linz), pp. 119–28.
4. Lawrence Kramer has recently commented on this reluctance in his essay 'Hugo Wolf: Subjectivity in the Fin-de-siècle Lied', in Rufus Hallmark, ed., *German Lieder in the Nineteenth Century* (New York, 1996), p. 186.
5. See, for example, Jean-Jacques Nattiez, *Wagner Androgyne*, tr. Stewart Spencer (Princeton, New Jersey, 1993). Also John Deathridge, 'Wagner and the Post-modern', *Cambridge Opera Journal*, 4 (1992), pp. 143–61.

1 'Music of the future'? The nature of the Wagnerian inheritance

1. Eduard Hanslick, *Die moderne Oper: aus neuer und neuester Zeit* (Berlin, 1900), p. 77.
2. See Hugo Wolf, *Briefe an Melanie Köchert*, ed. Franz Grasberger (Tutzing, 1964), p. 39.
3. See Ernst Decsey, 'Stunden mit Mahler', *Die Musik*, 40 (1911), p.114. These recorded comments of Mahler are discussed in Edward F. Kravitt, *The Lied, Mirror of Late Romanticism* (New Haven and London, 1996), p. 74.
4. See, for example, Henri-Louis de la Grange, *Mahler*, 2 vols. (London, 1974), vol. I, p. 290, quoting from Mahler's letter to his sister Justine where he says Strauss belongs to a 'bigoted and sanctimonious priesthood'.
5. See Richard Wagner, 'Beethoven', in *Gesammelte Schriften und Dichtungen*, 2nd edition, 10 vols. (Leipzig, 1887–8), vol. IX, pp. 134–5 (for English translation see *Richard Wagner's Prose Works*, ed. William Ashton Ellis, 8 vols. (London, 1891–9), vol. V, pp. 111–12). Also Wagner, 'Über die Benennung "Musikdrama"', *Gesammelte Schriften*, vol. IX, p. 364 (*Prose Works*, vol. V, p. 303).

6. See Wagner, 'Über das Opern-Dichten und -Komponieren im besonderen', *Gesammelte Schriften*, vol. X, pp. 226–7 (*Prose Works*, vol. VI, pp. 171–2).

7. See Hans von Wolzogen, ed., 'Richard Wagner und die Bayreuther Blätter – Erinnerungen und Mahnungen aus sechs Jahren für das Siebente', *Bayreuther Blätter*, 7 (1884), p. 6. Articles on Luther appeared in the journal in January 1881 and on Dürer in July/August 1888.

8. Friedrich Nietzsche, 'Richard Wagner in Bayreuth', *Untimely Meditations*, tr. R. J. Hollingdale (Cambridge, 1983), p. 217 (for German text see Friedrich Nietzsche, 'Richard Wagner in Bayreuth', *Werke*, 2nd edition, ed. Karl Schlechta, 3 vols. (Munich, 1960), vol I, p. 390).

9. Nietzsche, 'On the Uses and Disadvantages of History for Life', *Untimely Meditations*, pp. 62–3 ('Vom Nutzen und Nachteil der Historie', *Werke*, vol. I, pp. 213–14).

10. Richard Wagner, *Selected Letters*, ed. and tr. Stewart Spencer and Barry Millington (London, 1987), p. 269.

11. See Heinrich Werner, *Hugo Wolf und der Wiener akademische Wagner-Verein* (Regensburg, 1926), p. 9.

12. *Achtzehnter Jahresbericht des Wiener akademischen Wagnervereins für das Jahr 1890* (Vienna, 1891), p. 14 (included as an appendix to the 1891 issue of *Bayreuther Blätter*). Similar phrases appear in Josef Schalk's article 'Das Musikmachen in Wagner-Vereinen' from the *Neunzehnter Jahresbericht des Wiener akademische Wagnervereins für das Jahr 1891* (Vienna, 1892), pp. 21–2 (see the end of the 1892 issue of *Bayreuther Blätter*).

13. Nietzsche, 'Richard Wagner in Bayreuth', *Untimely Meditations*, p. 245 (see *Werke*, vol. I, p. 423).

14. *Ibid.*, p. 245 (*Werke*, vol. I, p. 424).

15. See Arthur Seidl, 'Hat Richard Wagner eine Schule hinterlassen?', *Deutsche Schriften für Literatur und Kunst*, vol. II/3 (Kiel and Leipzig, 1892), p. 4.

16. *Ibid.*, pp. 3–6.

17. *Ibid.*, p. 30.

18. Josef Schalk, 'Lichtblicke aus der Zeitgenossenschaft – Anton Bruckner', *Bayreuther Blätter*, 7 (1884), p. 334. Jean-Jacques Nattiez discusses the significance of the 'eternal feminine' for Wagner at length in *Wagner Androgyne*, p. 154.

19. Arthur Seidl, *Moderner Geist in der deutschen Tonkunst: Gedanken eines Kulturpsychologen um des Jahrhunderts Wende* (Berlin, 1900), pp. 123–4.

20. Friedrich von Hausegger, 'Vom Musikalisch-Erhabenen: Prolegomena zur Aesthetik der Tonkunst von Dr. Arthur Seidl', *Bayreuther Blätter*, 11 (1888), pp. 199–200.

21. See the press notice for Seidl's essay at the end of the October/November issue of *Bayreuther Blätter*, 15 (1892). Ernst Decsey refers to such press notices as coming from the editor, Hans von Wolzogen (see Decsey, *Hugo Wolf*, vol. III, p. 11).

22. See, for example, Ludwig Schemann, 'Über die Bedeutung der Ballade für unsere Zeit und Zukunft', *Bayreuther Blätter*, 20 (1897), pp. 37–8.

23. See Max Graf, *Wagner-Probleme und andere Studien* (Vienna, 1900), p. 80.

24. Elizabeth Förster-Nietzsche, *The Nietzsche–Wagner Correspondence*, tr. Caroline V. Kerr (London, 1922), p. 276.

25. *Ibid.*, pp. 271–2.

26. *Ibid.*, p. 280.

27. See Friedrich Nietzsche, 'The Case of Wagner', *The Birth of Tragedy and The Case of Wagner*, tr. Walter Kaufmann (New York, 1967), p. 186 ('Der Fall Wagner', *Werke*, vol. II, p. 933).

28. Graf, *Wagner-Probleme*, pp. 7–8.
29. *Ibid.*, p. 40.
30. *Ibid.*, p. 7.
31. *Ibid.*, pp. 70–1.
32. *Ibid.*, p. 86.
33. *Ibid.*, pp. 70–1.
34. *Ibid.*, p. 106. See Nietzsche, 'The Case of Wagner', p. 187 (*Werke*, vol. II, p. 934).
35. Graf, *Wagner-Probleme*, pp. 128–9.
36. *Ibid.*, pp. 132–3.
37. Theodor Adorno, *Mahler: A Musical Physiognomy*, tr. Edmund Jephcott (Chicago and London, 1971/1992), p. 39.
38. See Knud Martner, ed., *Selected Letters of Gustav Mahler*, tr. Eithne Wilkins, Ernst Kaiser and Bill Hopkins (London, 1979), p. 213.
39. Seidl, 'Hat Richard Wagner eine Schule hinterlassen?', p. 30.
40. Richard Wagner, 'Zukunftsmusik', *Gesammelte Schriften*, vol. VII, p. 171 (*Prose Works*, vol. III, p. 45).
41. Romain Rolland, *Correspondence, Diary and Essays*, ed. and tr. Rollo Myers (London, 1968), p. 120.
42. Nietzsche, 'The Case of Wagner', p. 156 (*Werke*, vol. II, p. 904).
43. *Ibid.*, p. 157 (*Werke*, vol. II, p. 905).
44. *Ibid.*, p. 188 (*Werke*, vol. II, p. 935).
45. Hans von Wolzogen, *Bayreuther Blätter*, 12 (1889); see the press notice at the end of the December issue.
46. Wolzogen, *Bayreuther Blätter*, 13 (1890); see the press notice for Wolf's Goethe songs at the end of the June issue.

2 'Wagner of the Lied'? Wolf as critic of Wagner and Wagnerism

1. See Frank Walker, *Hugo Wolf* (London, 1968), p. 157.
2. *Ibid.*, pp. 27–8.
3. See Hugo Wolf, *Familienbriefe*, ed. Edmund Hellmer (Leipzig, 1912), p. 5.
4. Walker, *Hugo Wolf*, p. 236, quoting from an unpublished letter to Wolf's mother.
5. *Ibid.*, p. 382, quoting from a letter from Wolf to Richard Sternfeld.
6. See Gustav Schur, *Erinnerungen an Hugo Wolf, nebst Hugo Wolfs Briefen an Gustav Schur*, ed. Heinrich Werner (Regensburg, 1922), p. 20.
7. Susan Youens, *Hugo Wolf: The Vocal Music* (Princeton, New Jersey, 1992). p. 4.
8. See, for example, Hugo Wolf, *Briefe an Oskar Grohe*, ed. Heinrich Werner (Berlin, 1905), pp. 13–16, and Hugo Wolf, *Briefe an Emil Kauffmann*, ed. Edmund Hellmer (Berlin, 1903), p. 12.
9. See Wolf, *Briefe an Kauffmann*, p. 104, and Werner, *Hugo Wolf und der Wiener akademische Wagner-Verein*, p. 87.
10. See Edmund Hellmer, *Hugo Wolf: Erlebtes und Erlauschtes* (Vienna and Leipzig, 1921), p. 130.
11. Hugo Wolf, *Music Criticism*, ed. and tr. Henry Pleasants (New York and London, 1978), p. 186.
12. See Decsey, *Hugo Wolf*, vol. III, pp. 1–3, and Theodor Helm, 'Fünfzig Jahre Wiener Musikleben', *Der Merker*, 8 (1917), pp. 275–6.
13. See Wolf, *Familienbriefe*, pp. 74–5.
14. See Werner, *Hugo Wolf und der Wiener akademische Wagner-Verein*, pp. 9–10.

15. The influence of Schalk's article in the *Münchener Allgemeine Zeitung*, 22 (1890) (included in Hugo Wolf-Verein in Wien, ed., *Gesammelte Aufsätze über Hugo Wolf*, vol. I, pp. 1–17) was recognised by many commentators. See, for example, Schur, *Erinnerungen an Hugo Wolf*, p. 15, and Decsey, *Hugo Wolf*, vol. III, p. 8.

16. Werner, *Hugo Wolf und der Wiener akademische Wagner-Verein*, p. 108.

17. Schur, *Erinnerungen an Hugo Wolf*, p. 17.

18. *Ibid.*, p. 19.

19. See Karl Heckel, *Hugo Wolf in seinem Verhältnis zu Richard Wagner* (Munich and Leipzig, 1905), p. 6.

20. Wolf, *Briefe an Kauffmann*, p. 114.

21. Wolf, *Music Criticism*, p. 127.

22. Ernest Newman, *Hugo Wolf* (London, 1907), p. 36.

23. Wolf, *Music Criticism*, p. 52.

24. Wolf, *Briefe an Köchert*, p. 194.

25. See Michael Haberlandt's preface to Hugo Wolf, *Briefe an Hugo Faisst*, ed. Michael Haberlandt (Stuttgart and Leipzig, 1904), p. 11. Also Rosa Mayreder's epilogue to Hugo Wolf, *Briefe an Rosa Mayreder*, ed. Heinrich Werner (Vienna, 1921), pp. 109, 113–14, and Wolf, *Briefe an Grohe*, p. 32.

26. Werner, *Hugo Wolf und der Wiener akademische Wagner-Verein*, p. 87.

27. *Ibid.*, pp. 53–6 (English translation taken from Walker, *Hugo Wolf*, pp. 218–19).

28. Walker, *Hugo Wolf*, p. 219.

29. See Wolf, *Briefe an Mayreder*, p. 111.

30. See Wolf, *Briefe an Grohe*, p. 242.

31. See Friedrich Eckstein, *Alte unnennbare Tage!* (Vienna, 1936), pp. 108–9.

32. *Ibid.*, p. 195.

33. *Ibid.*, pp. 195–6.

34. Wolf, *Briefe an Köchert*, p. 103, from a letter of 3 July 1894.

35. Eckstein, *Alte unnennbare Tage!*, p. 197.

36. See Wolf, *Briefe an Grohe*, pp. 30–1 (English translation taken from Walker, *Hugo Wolf*, p. 268).

37. See Franz Grasberger, *Hugo Wolf: Persönlichkeit und Werk: eine Ausstellung zum 100. Geburtstag* (Vienna, 1960), p. 74.

38. The examples are taken from the edition of the vocal score published by Peters (Leipzig, 1896).

39. See Wolf, *Briefe an Mayreder*, pp. 50–1.

40. Frank Walker suspected that the interchangeability of the two motifs was partly a matter of dramatic convenience, since from Act III scene 4 onwards Lukas and the Corregidor appear in each other's clothes (Walker, *Hugo Wolf*, p. 408).

41. Heckel, *Hugo Wolf in seinem Verhältnis zu Richard Wagner*, p. 7.

42. *Ibid.*, pp. 17–18.

43. Edmund Hellmer, 'Der Corregidor', in Hugo Wolf-Verein in Wien, ed., *Gesammelte Aufsätze über Hugo Wolf*, vol. I, p. 73.

44. See Hellmer's preface to *Der Corregidor von Hugo Wolf: kritische und biographische Beiträge zu seiner Würdigung*, ed. Edmund Hellmer (Berlin, 1900), p. 1.

45. See Heinrich Werner, *Der Hugo Wolf-Verein in Wien* (Regensburg, 1922), pp. 58–9.

46. *Ibid.*, pp. 28–9.

47. *Ibid.*, p. 24.

3 *Small things can also enchant us* – Wolf's challenge to nineteenth-century views of song

1. Wolf, *Briefe an Kauffmann*, pp. 55–6, from a letter of 12 October 1891.
2. Hugo Wolf, *Briefe an Heinrich Potpeschnigg*, ed. H. Nonveiller (Stuttgart, 1923), p. 37, from a letter of 16 May 1892.
3. Graf, *Wagner-Probleme*, p. 121.
4. See Friedrich von Hausegger, *Die Musik als Ausdruck* (Vienna, 1885).
5. Walter Niemann, *Die Musik seit Richard Wagner* (Berlin, 1913), p. 162.
6. See the thesis outlined by Marjorie Wing Hirsch in her book *Schubert's Dramatic Lieder* (Cambridge, 1993).
7. See *ibid.*, p. 7, quoting from Heinrich Christoph Koch, *Musikalisches Lexikon* (Frankfurt and Offenbach, 1802), pp. 901–4.
8. Hermann Kretzschmar, 'Das deutsche Lied seit dem Tode Richard Wagners', *Aufsätze aus den Jahrbüchern der Musikbibliothek Peters* (Leipzig, 1911), p. 285.
9. *Ibid.*, pp. 290–1.
10. See Berthold Litzmann, ed., *Clara Schumann – Johannes Brahms Briefe aus den Jahren 1853–1896* (Leipzig, 1927), p. 294.
11. See, for example, Gustav Jenner's accounts of Brahms's teaching and his insistence that his pupil learn from the absolute unity of the tonic key and surrounding relationships in simple strophic song (Gustav Jenner, 'Johannes Brahms as Man, Teacher and Artist', tr. Susan Gillespie in Walter Frisch, ed., *Brahms and His World* (Princeton, New Jersey, 1990), p. 198.
12. See Wagner, 'Oper und Drama', *Gesammelte Schriften*, vol. III, p. 308 (*Prose Works*, vol. II, pp. 39–40).
13. See Richard Wagner, 'Wilhelm Baumgartners Lieder', *Sämtliche Schriften und Dichtungen*, 16 vols. (Leipzig, 1911–16), vol. XII, pp. 285–6.
14. Heinrich Schuster, 'Die Verbindung von Musik und Poesie im Liede: zu Robert Franz' 75 Geburtstage', *Bayreuther Blätter*, 13 (1890), pp. 192–201.
15. Arthur Seidl, 'Erinnerungen an Robert Franz', *Wagneriana: erlebte Aesthetik*, 3 vols. (Berlin and Leipzig, 1901–2), vol. II, pp. 404–18.
16. *Ibid.*, p. 412.
17. Friedrich von Hausegger, *Frühe Schriften und Essays*, ed. Rudolf Flotzinger (Graz, 1986), pp. 96–7.
18. See, for example, Hans von Wolzogen's press notice for Sommer's *Werner's Lieder aus Welschland* at the end of the December issue of *Bayreuther Blätter*, 12 (1889).
19. Hans Sommer's *Lieder aus Julius Wolff's Minnesang Tannhäuser*, Op. 5 and *Sappho's Gesänge aus Carmen Sylva's Dichtung*, Op. 6 were published by Henry Litolff (Braunschweig, 1884).
20. Wilhelm Baumgartner, *Noch sind die Tage der Rosen*, published by Augener in the collection *Germania* (London, 1901).
21. Hans Sommer, *Hunold Sinuf aus Julius Wolff's Dichtung*, Op. 4 (Braunschweig, 1884).

4 'Poetry the man, music the woman'? Wolf's reworking in his Mörike songs of Wagner's aesthetics of words and music

1. See Josef Schalk, 'Neue Lieder, neues Leben', in Hugo Wolf-Verein in Wien, ed., *Gesammelte Aufsätze über Hugo Wolf*, vol. I, pp. 1–3.

2. Wagner, 'Oper und Drama', *Gesammelte Schriften*, vol. IV, pp. 183–4 and 199–201 (*Prose Works*, vol. II, pp. 285–6 and 299–301).
3. See, for example, Newman, *Hugo Wolf*, p. 187: 'When [Wolf] set Goethe he *was* Goethe.'
4. See Ernst Decsey, *Hugo Wolf: das Leben und das Lied* (Berlin, 1921), p. 147, quoting from Wolf's words to the composer Engelbert Humperdinck.
5. Nietzsche, 'The Case of Wagner', p. 167 (*Werke*, vol. II, p. 914).
6. Theodor Adorno, *In Search of Wagner*, tr. Rodney Livingstone (London, 1981), pp. 104–5.
7. *Ibid.*, pp. 91–2.
8. Nietzsche, 'The Case of Wagner', p. 159 (*Werke*, vol. II, p. 907).
9. Wolf, *Brief an Mayreder*, p. 82, from a letter of 16 June 1896.
10. See Hellmer, *Hugo Wolf: Erlebtes und Erlauschtes*, p. 136.
11. See Wolf, *Briefe an Grohe*, p. 37, from a letter of 3 September 1890.
12. See, for example, Hermann Kretzschmar, 'Das deutsche Lied seit Robert Schumann', *Gesammelte Aufsätze über Musik und Anderes aus den Grenzboten* (Leipzig, 1910), pp. 1–35.
13. See Walker, *Hugo Wolf*, p. 229.
14. Eric Sams, *The Songs of Hugo Wolf*, 2nd edition (London, 1983), p. 64.
15. See Walker, *Hugo Wolf*, pp. 202–3.

5 The integrity of musical language – questions of form and meaning in Wolf's Goethe songs

1. Seidl, *Moderner Geist in der deutschen Tonkunst*, pp. 126–7.
2. See J. P. Eckermann, *Conversations with Goethe*, ed. J. K. Moorhead, tr. John Oxenford (London, 1970), pp. 392–4.
3. *Ibid.*, p. 7.
4. *Ibid.*, p. 196.
5. Johann Wolfgang von Goethe, *From my Life: Poetry and Truth*, parts one to three, ed. Thomas P. Saine and Jeffrey L. Sammons, tr. Robert R. Heitner (New York, 1987), p. 358.
6. Michael Hamburger, *Beethoven: Letters, Journals and Conversations* (London, 1951), p. 89, as reported to Goethe by Bettina Brentano.
7. *Ibid.*, p. 223, from an account by Carl Czerny.
8. *Ibid.*, p. 88, as reported to Goethe by Bettina Brentano.
9. cf. Kravitt, *The Lied, Mirror of Late Romanticism*, p. 83, where he links such prevailing nineteenth-century Lieder aesthetics to Schopenhauer and Wagner.
10. See, for example, Walker, *Hugo Wolf*, p. 242.
11. See Harry E. Seelig, 'Goethe's "Buch Suleika" and Hugo Wolf: A Musico-Literary Study' (Ph.D. diss., University of Kansas, 1969), pp. 70–7.
12. See George Henry Lewes, *The Life of Goethe*, 3rd edition (London, 1875), p. 391.
13. cf. Lawrence Kramer, 'Decadence and Desire: The *Wilhelm Meister* Songs of Wolf and Schubert', *Nineteenth-Century Music*, 10 (1987), pp. 229–42.
14. Hamburger, *Beethoven*, pp. 88–9.
15. Wolf, *Briefe an Köchert*, p. 39.
16. Hugo Wolf, *Briefe an Frieda Zerny*, ed. Ernst Hilmar and Walter Obermaier (Vienna, 1978), p. 58.
17. Wolf, *Briefe an Kauffmann*, p. 8, from a letter of 21 May 1890.
18. Wolf, *Briefe an Grohe*, from a letter of 27 February 1897.
19. Sams, *The Songs of Hugo Wolf*, p. 199.

20. See Youens, *Hugo Wolf: The Vocal Music*, p. 105.
21. Johann Wolfgang von Goethe, *Wilhelm Meisters Lehrjahre* (Wilhelm Meister's Years of Apprenticeship), tr. H. M. Waidson, 6 vols. (London, 1977), vol. I, pp. 119–20.
22. *Ibid.*, vol. I, p. 120.
23. *Ibid.*, vol. II, p. 116.
24. Sams, *The Songs of Hugo Wolf*, p. 40.

6 The Wolfian perspective – comparisons with the songs of Strauss and Mahler

1. See Kravitt, *The Lied, Mirror of Late Romanticism*, p. 168.
2. See, for example, Adorno, *In Search of Wagner*, p. 43.
3. Kravitt, *The Lied, Mirror of Late Romanticism*, p. 191.
4. Adorno, *Mahler: A Musical Physiognomy*, p. 17.
5. *Ibid.*, p. 39.
6. See Donald Mitchell, *Gustav Mahler: The Wunderhorn Years* (London, 1975), pp. 27–8.
7. Graf, *Wagner-Probleme*, p. 7.

Bibliography

Musical editions

Mahler, Gustav, *Lieder eines fahrenden Gesellen*, Weinberger edition (London, 1946).
  Sieben Lieder, Philharmonia edition (Vienna, n.d.).
Sommer, Hans, *Hunold Sinuf aus Julius Wolff's Dichtung*, Op. 4 (Braunschweig, 1884).
  Lieder aus Julius Wolff's Minnesang Tannhäuser, Op. 5 (Braunschweig, 1884).
  Sappho's Gesänge aus Carmen Sylva's Dichtung, Op. 6 (Braunschweig, 1884).
  Der Meermann, eine nordische Legende in einem Aufzuge von Hans von Wolzogen, Op. 28 (Leipzig, 1895).
Strauss, Richard, *Gesamtausgabe*, ed. Franz Trenner, vol. I (London, 1964).
Wagner, Richard, *Tristan und Isolde*, Schirmer Opera Score Editions (New York and London, 1934).
Wolf, Hugo, *Gedichte von Eduard Mörike*, Peters edition (London, Frankfurt and New York, n.d.).
  Gedichte von Goethe, Peters edition (London, Frankfurt and New York, n.d.).
  Spanisches Liederbuch nach Paul Heyse und Emmanuel Geibel, Peters edition (London, Frankfurt and New York, n.d.).
  Italienisches Liederbuch nach Paul Heyse, Peters edition (London, Frankfurt and New York, n.d.).
  Der Corregidor, vocal score, Peters edition (Leipzig, 1896).

Books and articles

Adorno, Theodor, *In Search of Wagner*, tr. Rodney Livingstone (London, 1981).
  Mahler: A Musical Physiognomy, tr. Edmund Jephcott (Chicago and London, 1971/1992).
Batka, Richard, *Kranz: Gesammelte Blätter über Musik* (Leipzig, 1903).
Deathridge, John, 'Wagner and the Post-modern', *Cambridge Opera Journal*, 4 (1992), pp. 143–61.
Decsey, Ernst, *Hugo Wolf*, 4 vols. (Berlin and Leipzig, 1903–6).
  Hugo Wolf: das Leben und das Lied (Berlin, 1921).
de la Grange, Henri-Louis, *Mahler*, vol. I (London, 1974).
Eckermann, J. P., *Conversations with Goethe*, ed. J. K. Moorhead, tr. John Oxenford (London, 1970).
Eckstein, Friedrich, *Alte unnennbare Tage!* (Vienna, 1936).
Ellis, William Ashton, *Richard Wagner's Prose Works*, 8 vols. (London, 1891–9).
Förster-Nietzsche, Elizabeth, *The Nietzsche–Wagner Correspondence*, tr. Caroline V. Kerr (London, 1922).
Frisch, Walter, ed., *Brahms and His World* (Princeton, New Jersey, 1990).
Geyer, Hans-Herwig, *Hugo Wolfs Mörike-Vertonungen* (Kassel, 1991).
Glauert, Amanda, '"Wagner of the Lied"? The Artistic Identity of Hugo Wolf' (Ph.D. diss., University of London, 1990).

Goethe, Johann Wolfgang von, *Wilhelm Meisters Lehrjahre* (Wilhelm Meister's Years of Apprenticeship), tr. H. M. Waidson, 6 vols. (London, 1977).

    From my Life: Poetry and Truth, ed. Thomas P. Saine and Jeffrey L. Sammons, tr. Robert R. Heitner (New York, 1987).

Graf, Max, *Wagner-Probleme und andere Studien* (Vienna, 1900).

Grasberger, Franz, *Hugo Wolf: Persönlichkeit und Werk: eine Ausstellung zum 100. Geburtstag* (Vienna, 1960).

Hallmark, Rufus, ed., *German Lieder in the Nineteenth Century* (New York, 1996).

Hamburger, Michael, *Beethoven: Letters, Journals and Conversations* (London, 1951).

Hanslick, Eduard, *Die moderne Oper: aus neuer und neuester Zeit* (Berlin, 1900).

Hausegger, Friedrich von, *Frühe Schriften und Essays*, ed. Rudolf Flotzinger (Graz, 1986).

Heckel, Karl, *Hugo Wolf in seinem Verhältnis zu Richard Wagner* (Munich and Leipzig, 1905).

Hellmer, Edmund, ed., *Der Corregidor von Hugo Wolf: kritische und biographische Beiträge zu seiner Würdigung* (Berlin, 1900).

Hellmer, Edmund, *Erlebtes und Erlauschtes* (Vienna and Leipzig, 1921).

Helm, Theodor, 'Fünfzig Jahre Wiener Musikleben', *Der Merker*, 6–11 (Vienna), 1915–20.

Hirsch, Marjorie Wing, *Schubert's Dramatic Lieder* (Cambridge, 1993).

Kramer, Lawrence, 'Decadence and Desire: The *Wilhelm Meister* Songs of Hugo Wolf and Schubert', *Nineteenth-Century Music*, 10 (1987), pp. 229–42.

Kravitt, Edward F., *The Lied, Mirror of Late Romanticism* (New Haven and London, 1996).

Kretzschmar, Hermann, 'Das deutsche Lied seit Robert Schumann', *Gesammelte Aufsätze über Musik und Anderes aus den Grenzboten* (Leipzig, 1910), pp. 1–35.

    'Das deutsche Lied seit dem Tode Richard Wagners', *Aufsätze aus den Jahrbüchern der Musikbibliothek Peters* (Leipzig, 1911), pp. 23–39.

Large, David C. and William Weber, eds., *Wagnerism in European Culture and Politics* (New York and London, 1984).

Leibnitz, Thomas, 'Josef Schalk: ein Wagnerianer zwischen Anton Bruckner und Hugo Wolf', *Bruckner Jahrbuch 1980* (Linz), pp. 119–28.

Lewes, George Henry, *The Life of Goethe*, 3rd edition (London, 1875).

Litzmann, Berthold, ed., *Clara Schumann – Johannes Brahms Briefe aus den Jahren 1853–1896* (Leipzig, 1927).

Martner, Knud, ed., *Selected Letters of Gustav Mahler*, tr. Eithne Wilkins, Ernst Kaiser and Bill Hopkins (London, 1979).

Millington, Barry and Stewart Spencer, eds., *Wagner in Performance* (New Haven and London, 1992).

Mitchell, Donald, *Gustav Mahler: The Wunderhorn Years* (London, 1975).

Moos, Paul, *Richard Wagner als Ästhetiker: Versuch einer kritischen Darstellung* (Berlin and Leipzig, 1906).

Nattiez, Jean-Jacques, *Wagner Androgyne*, tr. Stewart Spencer (Princeton, New Jersey, 1992).

Newman, Ernest, *Hugo Wolf* (London, 1907).

Niemann, Walter, *Die Musik seit Richard Wagner* (Berlin, 1913).

Nietzsche, Friedrich, *Werke*, 2nd edition, ed. Karl Schlechta, 3 vols. (Munich, 1960).

    The Birth of Tragedy and The Case of Wagner, tr. Walter Kaufmann (New York, 1967).

    Untimely Meditations, tr. R. J. Hollingdale (Cambridge, 1983).

Rolland, Romain, *Correspondence, Diary and Essays*, ed. and tr. Rollo Myers (London, 1968).

Sams, Eric, *The Songs of Hugo Wolf*, 2nd edition (London, 1983).

Schorske, Carl, *Fin-de-siècle Vienna: Politics and Culture* (New York, 1981).

Schur, Gustav, *Erinnerungen an Hugo Wolf, nebst Hugo Wolfs Briefen an Gustav Schur*, ed. Heinrich Werner (Regensburg, 1922).

Seelig, Harry E., 'Goethe's "Buch Suleika" and Hugo Wolf: A Musico-Literary Study' (Ph.D. diss., University of Kansas, 1969).

Seidl, Arthur, 'Hat Richard Wagner eine Schule hinterlassen?', *Deutsche Schriften für Literatur und Kunst*, vol. II/3 (Kiel and Leipzig, 1892).

Moderner Geist in der deutschen Tonkunst: Gedanken eines Kulturpsychologen um des Jahrhunderts Wende (Berlin, 1900).

Wagneriana: erlebte Aesthetik, 3 vols. (Berlin and Leipzig, 1901–2).

Siegel, Linda, *Music in German Romantic Literature* (Novato, California, 1983).

Stein, Deborah, *Hugo Wolf's Lieder and Extensions of Tonality* (Ann Arbor, Michigan, 1985)

Stein, Jack, *Poem and Music in the German Lied from Gluck to Hugo Wolf* (Cambridge, Massachusetts, 1971).

Stoljar, Margaret Mahony, *Poetry and Song in Late Eighteenth-century Germany* (London, 1985).

Wagner, Richard, *Gesammelte Schriften und Dichtungen*, 2nd edition, 10 vols. (Leipzig, 1887–8).

Sämtliche Schriften und Dichtungen, 16 vols. (Leipzig, 1911–16).

Selected Letters, ed. and tr. Stewart Spencer and Barry Millington (London, 1987).

Walker, Frank, *Hugo Wolf* (London, 1968).

Werner, Heinrich, *Der Hugo Wolf-Verein in Wien* (Regensburg, 1922).

Hugo Wolf und der Wiener akademische Wagner-Verein (Regensburg, 1926).

Wiora, Walter, *Das deutsche Lied: zur Geschichte und Ästhetik einer musikalischen Gattung* (Wolfenbüttel and Zurich, 1971).

Wolf, Hugo, *Briefe an Emil Kauffmann*, ed. Edmund Hellmer (Berlin, 1903).

Briefe an Hugo Faisst, ed. Michael Haberlandt (Stuttgart and Leipzig, 1904).

Briefe an Oskar Grohe, ed. Heinrich Werner (Berlin, 1905).

Familienbriefe, ed. Edmund Hellmer (Leipzig, 1912).

Briefe an Rosa Mayreder, ed. Heinrich Werner (Vienna, 1921).

Briefe an Heinrich Potpeschnigg, ed. H. Nonveiller (Stuttgart, 1923).

Briefe an Melanie Köchert, ed. Franz Grasberger (Tutzing, 1964).

Briefe an Frieda Zerny, ed. Ernst Hilmar and Walter Obermaier (Vienna, 1978).

Music Criticism, ed. and tr. Henry Pleasants (New York and London, 1978).

Hugo Wolf-Verein in Wien, ed., *Gesammelte Aufsätze über Hugo Wolf*, 2 vols. (Berlin, 1898).

Wolzogen, Hans von, ed., *Bayreuther Blätter* (Chemnitz, 1878–1938).

Youens, Susan, *Hugo Wolf: The Vocal Music* (Princeton, New Jersey, 1992).

Index

⬦⬦⬦

Page numbers in bold type refer to discussions which include musical examples.